The Antarctic
and Patagonia

MANAGING EDITORS
Amy Bauman
Barbara J. Behm

CONTENT EDITORS
Amanda Barrickman
James I. Clark
Patricia Lantier
Charles P. Milne, Jr.
Katherine C. Noonan
Christine Snyder
Gary Turbak
William M. Vogt
Denise A. Wenger
Harold L. Willis
John Wolf

ASSISTANT EDITORS
Ann Angel
Michelle Dambeck
Barbara Murray
Renee Prink
Andrea J. Schneider

INDEXER
James I. Clark

ART/PRODUCTION
Suzanne Beck, Art Director
Andrew Rupniewski, Production Manager
Eileen Rickey, Typesetter

Library of Congress Number: 88-18337

2   3   4   5   6   7   8   9   0   97   96   95   94   93   92

Library of Congress Cataloging-in-Publication Data

Boitani, Luigi.
  [Antartide e Patagonia. English]
  The Antarctic and Patagonia / Luigi Boitani, Stefania
Bartoli, Laura Beani.

  — (World nature encyclopedia)
  Translation of: Antartide e Patagonia.
  Includes index.
  Summary: Describes the natural and ecological niches,
boundaries, and life of the wildlife habitats of the Antarctic
and Patagonia.
  1. Ecology—Antarctic regions—Juvenile literature.
2. Ecology—Patagonia (Argentina and Chile) 3. Biotic
communities—Antarctic regions—Juvenile literature.
4. Biotic communities—Patagonia (Argentina and Chile)
[Ecology—Antarctic regions. 2. Ecology—Patagonia
(Argentina and Chile) 3. Biotic communities—Antarctic
regions. 4. Biotic communities—Patagonia (Argentina and
Chile)] I. Bartoli, Stefania. II. Beani, Laura, 1955-.
Title. IV. Series: Natura nel mondo. English.
  QH84.1.B6513   1988   574.5′2621′0998—dc19   88-18364
  ISBN 0-8172-3325-3

WORLD NATURE ENCYCLOPEDIA

The Antarctic and Patagonia

Luigi Boitani
Stefania Bartoli
Laura Beani

RAINTREE
STECK-VAUGHN
L I B R A R Y

Austin, Texas

CONTENTS

INTRODUCTION

The Antarctic makes up about one-tenth of the total area of the earth. Yet despite its large size, the region has received little attention and recognition from the general public. Of course, there is little variety in the environments of Antarctica. Only sparse populations of plants and animals are found there. Few people reside in the area, and most are scientists. Nevertheless, the climate and oceans of Antarctica strongly influence the whole Southern Hemisphere and, to some extent, the Northern Hemisphere as well.

Antarctica is rich in mineral deposits and certain marine resources. The fresh water trapped within the ice of Antarctica accounts for 90 percent of all the fresh water on earth. Its land environments are of a scale unequaled anywhere else in the world. It is the coldest and most isolated continent. Winds there reach the highest speeds ever encountered on earth. The antarctic seas are also among the stormiest. Nevertheless, the beauty of its environments is unique.

Many people believe that the Antarctic is totally unfit for life. This is because humans have a tendency to look at the surrounding world from a viewpoint of how it relates to them. Antarctica is often considered a barren land, with an impossible or extreme environment. Actually, a considerable number of plant and animal species inhabits the area. They are perfectly adapted to that environment, and some thrive only there.

The Antarctic is still little known even to scientists. Only in recent years have scientists begun to gather information in an organized way. They have done studies on various subjects. These subjects range from animals to meteorology (the science dealing with atmospheric phenomena such as weather). This research does not seem to be totally without self-interest, however. There is a well-founded suspicion that all the nations supporting research in the Antarctic hope to profit from it someday. Nations are suspected of spending their research funds in order to be the first to take advantage of the Antarctic's resources. This unfortunate competition is, nevertheless, bringing about new scientific discoveries in a land that is still relatively untouched.

More is known about the sea than the land. Seal hunters and whalers were the first to discover the Antarctic coasts. They tried to obtain the maximum profit from the resources they found there. These hunters almost completely destroyed the populations of several sea animals.

HISTORY

The Antarctic is unique. Its structure and environment are very different from those of any other area, including the Arctic. The area has no history of colonization. Nor is there any record of human cultures. The history of the Antarctic is recent, and the people who made this history were spurred on by the spirit of adventure, scientific curiosity, or greed.

Antarctic explorers encountered extreme climatic and environmental conditions. In a certain sense, these conditions can be compared to the situation encountered by the first astronauts who landed on the moon. The strange landscape of the Antarctic could well serve as the setting for a science fiction movie.

Discovery and the First Expeditions

The Antarctic is the last continent to have been discovered; the ancient Greeks were the first to have theorized its existence. Centuries before Christ, the Greeks believed the earth was a sphere. They had heard of the existence of cold lands near the Arctic Circle and reasoned that a land at the South Pole was necessary to balance the far northern lands. They called this land *terra incognita australis*, which means "unknown southern land." But the theory of its existence was not popular until the voyages of Christopher Columbus proved that the earth was, indeed, round. From that point on, the mapmakers began to draw this unknown southern land on their maps.

Captain James Cook was the first European to sail in Antarctic waters in 1772. Cook, as well as others, was looking for the unknown continent of Antarctica. However, Nathaniel Palmer, a seal hunter from Connecticut, was actually the first person to see its coasts. Although he was unaware of what he had seen, Palmer had sailed as far south as the Antarctic Peninsula in 1829. Other seal and whale hunters reached these southern latitudes later, while also looking for new hunting areas.

Due to the explorations of such hunters, the theory of the existence of lands at the South Pole became more and more concrete. Between 1830 and 1840, there were numerous scientific discoveries. For example, the first sample of fossil wood was collected by James Eights, a naturalist on Palmer's ship. Eights brought back many specimens from the Antarctic voyage, including such things as lichens, rocks, and vertebrate and invertebrate animals. Vertebrate animals are those that have a backbone, while invertebrate animals do not.

Preceding pages: A group of penguins rests on a flat iceberg in Antarctica.

Opposite page: A ship approaches Stonington Island, west of the Antarctic Peninsula. The wind blowing from the higher land makes beautiful ripples on the ocean's surface.

Mount Erebus rises from Ross Island. In the foreground are drifting fragments of the pack ice.

A strong economic and scientific interest in the southern land had been aroused. The economic interest almost always came before the scientific, as in the case of seal hunting. After the first definite reports of the new continent's existence, several countries began to organize expeditions to explore the land. France began with Jules Dumont d'Urville in 1837. The United States organized the expedition of Charles Wilkes (1838), and Great Britain sent James Clark Ross (1839-1841). The expeditions were organized for exploratory and scientific purposes, and each party sought to plant its country's flag on the new territory.

The economic interest was the driving factor. In the majority of cases, only small amounts of money were available to engage scientists, and on every expedition the naturalist on board was a secondary figure. The naturalist was often the only person responsible for studying animals,

plants, rocks, and minerals, as well as the weather and other atmospheric phenomena.

On the Ross expedition, this job fell to Joseph Hooker, a medical doctor. Hooker brought back an enormous amount of material for study. Once back in England, he began to carefully classify all of it, and, in 1847, he published a book on the antarctic plants. In this volume, Hooker described the system used in classifying the samples. He also included a comparison of the antarctic plants with the plants of South America and Australia.

Ross's expedition, using two well-equipped ships, was a great success for England. The expedition discovered a large bay close to the south magnetic pole. They named it the Ross Sea. The party also sailed in the Weddel Sea, which had been named for James Weddell, a British seal hunter and the bay's discoverer. The Ross expedition is also credited with discovering Mount Erebus, which is a large, active volcano, and the Ross Ice Shelf, which is a large ice barrier that covers the southern half of the sea. The expedition set a new record by reaching 78° 9′ south latitude.

American naturalist T. Ramsey Peale, a member of the 1838 Wilkes party, was not as lucky. The purpose of his six-ship expedition sent by the United States was mainly exploratory, although there was a clear intention to establish American sovereignty in Antarctica. While plagued by numerous difficulties, Wilkes navigated through the icy waters closest to the south magnetic pole. He sighted a "very long coastline," which he followed for 1,500 miles (2,500 kilometers). This confirmed that the land in question was truly a continent. Peale collected specimens of birds and sea animals, making notes of all observations in a journal. Unfortunately, all the samples he collected were lost in a shipwreck during the return voyage.

The interest in the Antarctic for science and adventure was rekindled in the 1890s. In the meantime, economic interest in the still-unknown land had continued. The abundance of whales and fur seals in the southern seas attracted a great number of hunters. Driven by the sizable profits made by the first whalers in the area, hunters began to kill a tremendous number of seals and whales. They subjected themselves to living conditions that were often extremely difficult. The companies they worked for directed the operations from much more comfortable bases.

The crew of a seal hunting ship would find a particularly favorable area where many animals had gathered. The

Sleds used by the antarctic explorers in the early part of the twentieth century were equipped with large metal runners. In those years, the scientists of the well-equipped expeditions brought back a great deal of information on the natural sciences from Antarctica.

party would then kill as many as the ship could carry back to a base. Setting out for home with furs and meat, the hunters would leave some crew members behind as guards to watch over the plentiful hunting area and make sure ships of other companies did not enter it. These people spent the winter in the cold of the subantarctic islands while waiting for their ship to return. They lived in huts built from lumber that the ships had brought, and they burned dried bog moss for heat. Their food consisted of smoked fish and seal meat.

During these hunting trips, there was no interest on the part of commanders to make notes of locations visited or things they had found there. The discovery of a group of small islands, for example, had no importance for them, unless the islands were the site of a large seal colony. In that case, they would remain silent about the existence of the islands until all of the seals living there were killed.

From the *Challenger* to the Heroic Explorations

The British *Challenger* expedition was an exception to the lack of scientific interest in the Antarctic between 1840 and 1880. Guided by Charles Thomson, a professor of natural history at the University of Edinburgh, Scotland, the *Challenger* sailed in 1872 on a voyage that reached 65° south latitude and lasted 3½ years. The expedition gathered numerous examples of unknown marine animals, detailed information on the ocean, and collections of land animals and plants of the subantarctic islands. The information was compiled into fifty volumes, which represented a complete report of the long expedition.

Not until 1895 did someone finally succeed in landing on the continent. He was Carsten Borchgrevink, a Norwegian, who also climbed the headland (a point of unusually high land jutting out into a body of water) at the entrance of the Ross Sea. Encouraged by this success, Borchgrevink returned to Antarctica in 1897 and was the first to spend a winter on land. In the same year, Roald Amundsen headed a Belgian expedition that spent the winter on a glacier off the Antarctic coast.

Several scientists participated in Borchgrevink's expedition. William Colbek studied magnetism, L. Bernacchi observed atmospheric phenomena and weather, and N. Hanson studied biology. Unfortunately, Hanson died during the expedition. The only remains of his work were his notebook of observations, and several specimens of fish,

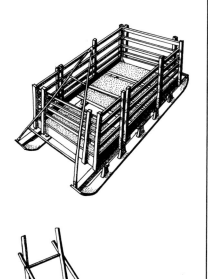

sponges, sea squirts, starfish, sea urchins, sea cucumbers, mollusks (such as clams, snails, and squid), and corals.

A series of great explorations characterized the twentieth century. Various attempts were made to reach locations where humans had never set foot before, and the South Pole was one of these. By this time, many of the problems related to the North Pole had been solved or were about to be solved, and the scientific world became deeply interested in information coming from the Antarctic. The general public closely followed the discoveries of the new land, and many expeditions to the South Pole were financed solely by private groups of people.

During the first half of the twentieth century, the approach to the Antarctic continent became more and more heroic as well as scientific. People like Roald Amundsen, Robert Scott, and Richard Byrd became legendary figures. Regular scientific expeditions were organized by various nations, beginning with a British expedition in 1901. This British expedition embarked with the *Discovery* under the command of Scott. Highly qualified and well-equipped

Several sled dogs wait to transport materials just unloaded from an airplane on Anvers Island, west of the Antarctic Peninsula. The materials and supplies are to be used at a research base. In Antarctica, there are thirty-two operating scientific bases that belong to twelve nations.

scientists participated in the voyage. They collected a large amount of information, especially on geology (the science of the earth's structure), birds, and plants. Ernest Shackleton also participated in this expedition, and the voyage represented important "training" during which he and Scott experimented with different systems of exploring the cold and icy lands.

Shackleton returned to the Antarctic during 1907-1909 with another expedition. It was successful only from a scientific viewpoint. The party made important discoveries about the structure and evolution of the land formations and the composition of its rocks. An Australian scientist

succeeded in planting the British flag at the south magnetic pole. Shackleton, however, was not as fortunate. He left the base intending to reach the geographic South Pole. By January 9, 1909, after having overcome great difficulties, he had arrived at a point only 99 miles (160 km) from his goal. Because of insufficient food and supplies, however, he had to turn back. Had he continued, the entire crew would have died from cold and hunger on the return trip.

About a year later, in December 1911, the Norwegian Amundsen succeeded where Shackleton had failed. He planted the Norwegian flag at the geographic South Pole. The Briton Robert Scott, who returned to the Antarctic at the same time as Amundsen, was also intent on reaching the pole. Arriving there, Scott discovered that Amundsen had preceded him by a month. Discouraged, he and his four companions began their ill-fated return to the base. One died after a fall and another from venturing out into a storm. Scott and the other two froze to death in a tent while waiting out a storm. Ironically, they were just 10 miles (16 km) from safety.

In 1914, Great Britain once more sent its foremost Antarctic explorer, Shackleton, as commander of an expedition. The objective of this expedition was to cross the entire continent, from the Weddell Sea to the Ross Sea. However, this venture was not successful. Upon entering the Weddell Sea, where the base was to be established, the ship was obstructed by ice. They launched a lifeboat and reached Elephant Island on April 15, 1916.

Next came the era of airplane expeditions, of which Richard Byrd of the United States was the champion. During a 1928-1929 trip, Byrd established the so-called Little America base in the area of the Ross Sea. From here, the American explorer took off in a three-engine plane and covered the 1,597 miles (2,570 km) to the pole and back in a single day. Byrd's excursions were not limited to exploration by airplane. He also set off with sleds to establish a meteorological station 124 miles (200 km) from the base. This station measured the weather and atmospheric conditions automatically. Byrd returned to the Antarctic in 1934 and again in 1939 and in 1947. He gathered a great amount of information on atmospheric phenomena and the mechanical properties of rock layers. He also mapped the coastline and mountainous reliefs from above the continent. Byrd devoted much of his life to the exploration of Antarctica. He made many important scientific discoveries there.

GEOGRAPHY

All of the 5,326,800 square miles (13.8 million square kilometers) of Antarctica are located within the Southern Hemisphere. Antarctica is separated from other continents by vast polar oceans, and it is almost entirely covered by ice. Antarctica has a nearly circular shape, with its center at the South Pole. The maximum diameter of this near circle is 2,485 miles (4,000 km), and its circumference is 19,822 miles (31,900 km).

This almost perfectly round shape is altered by the presence of the Antarctic Peninsula and two huge bays, the Ross Sea and the Weddell Sea. The Antarctic Peninsula is a tongue of land that extends toward South America. Most of the area of the Ross and Weddell seas is occupied by permanent ice. The trans-Antarctic Mountains extend from the Weddell Sea to the Ross Sea. They divide Antarctica into two parts—the western and the eastern regions.

The eastern part, which faces the Indian Ocean, makes up two-thirds of the continent. Here the ice is thicker than on the western part, which faces the Pacific Ocean. This western area includes the Antarctic Peninsula and the highest mountains. These are the Ellsworth Mountains and the Vinson Massif.

Ice, the Undisputed Master

Antarctica is nearly all ice. Only about 2 percent of the area, or about 96,525 sq. miles (250,000 sq. km) is free of ice. The zones not covered by the ice sheet, or cap, have a bare rock surface. They are found on the Antarctic Peninsula, Coats Land, Queen Maud Land, the Mac-Robertson Coast, and the Ellsworth Mountains.

Most of the rock outcroppings resemble reefs and are called "nunataks." These are actually the peaks of mountains that lie mostly beneath the ice and snow. The ice cannot accumulate on the nunataks because they are very steep.

Certain zones of the Antarctic are called "oases" because of their favorable climatic conditions. In several parts of the continent, they extend for hundreds of miles. The bare rock in these areas absorbs the sun's radiation during the summer months. This radiation is then released into the air, which causes the temperature to rise. In the warmest hours of the day, the temperature can reach up to 59°F (15°C). This prevents the formation of ice on the rocks.

The landscape of the oases reminds one of the extraterrestrial landscapes photographed by space probes. Because

Opposite page: Ice forms a large wall in Antarctica. The ice is the supreme master of this continent, covering about 98 percent of its surface. The volume of antarctic ice is about 6.5 million cubic miles (30 million cu. km) and makes up 80 percent of all the fresh water on the planet.

17

of the alternate freezing and thawing, the land becomes eroded and is slowly eaten away. Layers flake off the rocks, creating peculiar forms. However, these environments are exceptions to the structure of the great majority of Antarctica. The undisputed master of this continent is the ice, which covers 98 percent of the continent's surface. The total volume occupied by the Antarctic ice cap has been estimated at about 6.5 million cubic miles (30 million cubic km). This represents about 80 percent of all the fresh water in the world.

The average thickness of the ice is 1 mile (2 km), but at its highest point the ice reaches an elevation of 2 miles (4 km) above sea level. If all this ice were to melt (which would require thousands of years), the sea level around the world would rise by about 197 feet (60 meters).

Antarctic ice originated from the accumulation of snow over the course of hundreds of thousands of years.

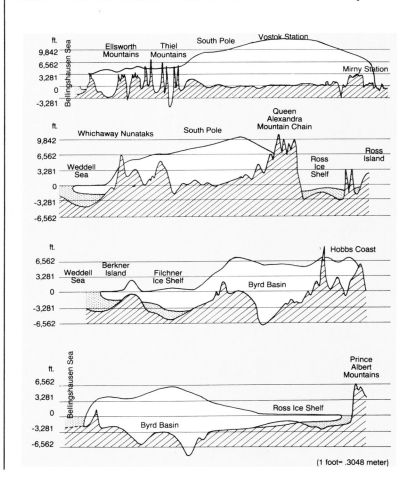

Four different sections across the antarctic ice cap. Several mountain peaks exceed the elevation of 9,842 feet (3,000 m). The ice reaches a thickness of 13,123 feet (4,000 m). The enormous weight of the ice mass presses down the underlying rock masses to 3,281 to 6,562 feet (1,000 to 2,000 m) below sea level. In the sections, the continental mass is indicated with diagonal lines, while the ice mass is shown in white. The seawater is shown with dots.

(1 foot= .3048 meter)

Year after year, the existing layers of snow are covered by new layers. This process continues until, at a depth of 328 feet (100 m), the weight of the snow pressing down from above changes the lower snow into ice. At this stage, the ice begins a slow, downward movement to the rock base. This movement starts in the interior and gradually reaches the sea. At several points in flatter areas, the ice advances at a speed of about 7 feet (2 m) per year. But as it nears the coast, it can reach a speed of .62 miles (1 km) per year.

After having found a path to the sea, the large blocks of ice move beyond the submerged coastline into the open sea. In the Ross Sea, the sheet of ice moving from the continent forms a huge platform called the Ross Ice Shelf. This extends 497 miles (800 km) beyond the edge of the land before breaking up into flat-topped, or tabular, icebergs. These icebergs then begin to drift toward the north, gradually melting in the process. Icebergs as big as 62 miles (100 km) long and 31 miles (50 km) wide have been seen, but normally their dimensions are smaller.

Under the enormous layer of ice lies the land, with its mountains, valleys, and plains. In many zones, the land is below sea level; and, in some areas, the boundary between rock and ice is located at amazing depths. For example, in the Byrd Basin, the boundary reaches a depth of 8,202 feet (2,500 m). This situation is caused by the enormous weight of the ice (27,000 billion tons), which compresses the land and lowers it by about 1,968 feet (600 m).

If all of this ice were to melt, a large part of the continent would be covered by the ocean's water, and it would appear much smaller. The western region would look like an enormous plain, while the eastern region would consist of small islands.

The Great Climatic Changes

The theory of the movement of the earth's crust is known as "plate tectonics." According to the theory, 570 million years ago all the lands of the world were united into two enormous supercontinents. The continent in the Southern Hemisphere was called "Gondwanaland." It included the lands that now make up South America, Africa, India, New Zealand, Australia, and Antarctica. At that time, Antarctica was located in the same area as it is today, while the other continents were all joined around it.

About 130 million years ago, South America and Africa separated from this huge land mass and slowly began drift-

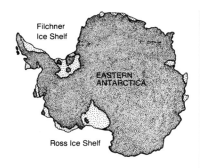

Filchner
Ice Shelf

EASTERN
ANTARCTICA

Ross Ice Shelf

EASTERN
ANTARCTICA

Shown are the present map of Antarctica *(top)* and the theoretical map of the continent if all of its ice were to melt completely *(bottom)*. If this occurred, all of the regions below sea level would be covered with water. The emerged surface would be considerably decreased, and the Antarctic Peninsula would become the largest island of the area. However, the melting of the ice would free the underlying rock from an enormous weight. As a result, the rock would rise up somewhat and balance out the new situation.

ing northward. Only the southern tip of South America remained attached to the supercontinent. Twenty-five million years ago, it separated for good.

Fossil evidence indicates that about 50 million years ago, Antarctica was free from ice. This evidence is represented by fossil wood, which suggests the presence of vast conifer forests and warmer climates in the past. But about 35 million years ago, the climate began to change. It was at this stage that the ice sheet began to form in the Antarctic because of a sharp decrease in temperature.

The advance and retreat of the ice at the edges of the ice cap have been reconstructed with precision for the last hundreds of thousands of years. Thus, it is known that the ice retreated suddenly about 124,000 years ago. On the other hand, the ice reached its maximum extension about 17,000 to 18,000 years ago. At that time, the continental glaciers advanced, along with the ice that originated in the sea. The ice, in fact, expanded and covered over 10 million sq. miles (26 million sq. km) of the southern seas. The thawing process, which started 14,000 years ago with the warming of the atmosphere, has led to the present extension of the ice cap.

Freezing Temperatures, Winds, Dryness, and Blizzards

The Antarctic is the coldest continent on earth. Incredibly extreme temperatures are reached. The Russian station at Vostok recorded a temperature of -129°F (-89.6°C) on July 21, 1983. The climate is also characterized by strong winds, extreme dryness, and frequent blizzards. During the blizzards, the visibility can drop to less than 3 feet (1 m).

These conditions are the result of a combination of circumstances. The first circumstance is the geographic position of this continent. As in the Arctic polar zone, winter nights last for several months and so do summer days. The sun sets in March and does not rise again until September. From September to March, the sun is always above the horizon. (At the North Pole, just the opposite occurs.)

The reason for this is well known. The axis around which the earth rotates is tilted with respect to the orbit in which it revolves around the sun. In the Southern Hemisphere, winter sets in when the northern areas are inclined toward the sun. During this time, Antarctica is enclosed in complete darkness. In the summer, when the earth is at the opposite point of its orbit, the region of the South Pole is

Lens-shaped clouds gather over the South Orkney Islands. The sky above the ice cap contains very dry atmospheric layers. This is partly due to the elevation of the land. The sparse clouds provide a minimum amount of precipitation. Furthermore, they do not hold in the sun's warmth. The radiation from the sun is lost through the clouds out into space. Almost everywhere in Antarctica, the temperatures are below 32°F (0°C) throughout the year.

inclined toward the sun. This causes the continent to be exposed to the sun for a long period of time.

The orbit of the earth around the sun is elliptical. That is, it is not perfectly round. At the moment of the December solstice (winter solstice in the Northern Hemisphere, summer solstice in the Southern Hemisphere), the earth is at its shortest distance from the sun (88 million miles, 147 million km). At the June solstice (summer in the North, winter in the South), the distance between the earth and the sun is the greatest (91 million miles, 152 million km). The difference between these distances influences the amount of solar radiation the earth receives. The solar radiation at the South Pole is 6.7 percent less than at the North Pole.

The already scarce solar radiation is further reduced by the phenomenon of reflectance. The enormous white surface of the ice reflects up to 90 percent of the sun's heat back into space. Solar radiation is less intense at the poles than at any other point on earth. This is caused by the fact that the rays are slanted when they reach the polar areas. Furthermore, the northern ice cap has more water vapor.

Pictured is the Ross Ice Shelf. The Antarctic continent can be called a "desert," since the annual precipitation, which is all in the form of snow, never exceeds 5 inches (130 mm). Nevertheless, the ice has accumulated over thousands of years, reaching spectacular proportions and power.

When the ice thaws, the area is covered by layers of low clouds. Over the southern ice cap, there are very dry cloud layers, partially due to its elevation. These layers do not act as a barrier, and the sun's heat is radiated back into space. As a result, all the infrared radiation of the sun passes back into space, making the climate colder.

Having been cooled on the highland, air masses move downward and toward the coast. They tend to move in a counterclockwise rotation. At the center of the continent, the air is relatively calm and very cold. Meanwhile, on the rest of the continent, especially near the coast, the winds reach a tremendous speed. Some may reach 186 miles (300 km) per hour. They last a long time and are characterized by quick changes in speed. Within a few minutes, relatively calm atmospheric conditions can change. The air masses can pick up a speed of 164 feet (50 m) per second. They can also lose speed that rapidly. Wind speed decreases considerably only a few miles away from the coast.

As mentioned earlier, the Antarctic temperatures are

the planet's coldest. On the highland, the monthly winter averages can drop to -94°F (-70°C) and beyond. Generally, near the coast, the temperatures are similar to those of the Arctic. They range from -4° to -40°F (-20° to -40°C). In the summer, the sun thaws the snow near certain rocks and forms several shallow pools of meltwater. In any month of the year, the average temperature does not rise above 32°F (0°C), except on the Antarctic Peninsula.

The coldest point of Antarctica is called the "pole of relative inaccessibility." It is located about 404 miles (650 km) from the geographic South Pole. It is so high, at 13,123 feet (4,000 m), and so cold that the air cannot contain much water vapor. The average snowfall on the continent does not exceed 5 inches (13 centimeters) per year.

Besides the "pole of relative inaccessibility," there are three other poles. The best known of these is the geographic South Pole. This is an imaginary point on the earth through which the earth's rotational axis passes.

While the geographic poles are fixed points on the land surface, the magnetic poles are not. The magnetic poles are located at the two points on the earth where a compass needle points downward. At these points, the lines of the magnetic field are vertical. Presently, the magnetic south pole is located at about 66° south latitude and 140° east longitude. This point is about 1,616 miles (2,600 km) from the geographic South Pole.

There are also the north and south geomagnetic poles. These are used by scientists to describe the basic magnetic fields of the earth. Magnetic poles and geomagnetic poles do not correspond. This is because other magnetic fields of the earth cause the surface magnetic fields to be different from the theoretic geomagnetic poles. The geomagnetic south pole is located on the highland of eastern Antarctica, where the Soviet base of Vostok is found.

The Antarctic Convergence

The ocean around Antarctica is composed of the southernmost parts of the Atlantic, Indian, and Pacific oceans. The climatic boundaries of Antarctica represent a line called the "Antarctic Convergence." This is the line where cold water currents coming from the south meet warm water currents coming from the north. The location of the line changes according to nearby lands. It also varies in relation to the features of the ocean bottom. These factors influence the movements of masses of water toward the north.

THE LAND ENVIRONMENT

Only 2 percent of the more than 5 million sq. miles (14 million sq. km) of land in Antarctica is ice free. It is somewhat difficult to imagine the land environment with its own identity. The extreme climatic conditions of Antarctica have resulted in the evolution of highly specialized life forms. Their most fascinating characteristics, other than the mechanisms of adaptation to cold, are simplicity and fragility.

The food chain of the various land organisms is characterized by a minimum number of energy transfers. The nutrition of some organisms is sometimes interrupted for long periods of time by the extreme weather. Usually, when food chains are simple, they are also fragile.

The first limiting factor for life in these environments is not related to the low temperatures but rather to the dryness. The water is usually completely trapped in a solid state of ice crystals. Only a small amount of water is available in the liquid state for thirsty land organisms. The second limiting factor is the lack of easily utilized nutrients. There is practically no soil with organic matter, and the surface waters are not able to carry nutrients to the few lakes free of ice.

The Plants

The land environments in Antarctica can be divided into three large areas, or bands, according to the type of vegetation and climate found in each of them. The outermost band is called the subantarctic band. It includes all the islands found in the region of the Convergence, between 55 and 46 degrees latitude south. The second area, called the "maritime band," includes the Antarctic Peninsula and several islands toward the east as far as Bouvetoya. The last band, which is the continental band, includes the greater part of the Antarctic land mass.

Although they are located next to each other, the maritime and continental bands are notably different. For example, in the summer, the average monthly temperature in the maritime band is 32° to 35.6°F (0° to 2°C); and in the winter, it rarely goes below 5°F (-15°C). In the continental band, the average monthly temperature always remains below 32°F (0°C) in the summer; while in the winter months, it generally drops below -13°F (-25°C).

Furthermore, the maritime zone receives between 10 and 40 inches (25 and 100 cm) of precipitation in the form of free water, while the continental zone receives only snow precipitation. The snow cover shields the vegetation from

Opposite page: An expanse of mosses and lichens covers a section of King George Island in the Shetlands. In the foreground, several bones, probably of a sea lion, can be seen. The ice-free lands of the Antarctic are inhabited by a community of highly-specialized land organisms. They are able to survive with minimum amounts of water and nutrients.

The so-called antarctic plant zone has very extreme characteristics. Mosses, fungi, lichens, and liverworts are almost the only plants that grow in this zone. The lichens can be found even at latitudes of over 85 degrees south. Interesting plant communities form in certain warmer places called "oases." (1. flowering plants; 2. blue-green algae; 3. bacteria and fungi; 4. lichens; 5. mosses and liverworts)

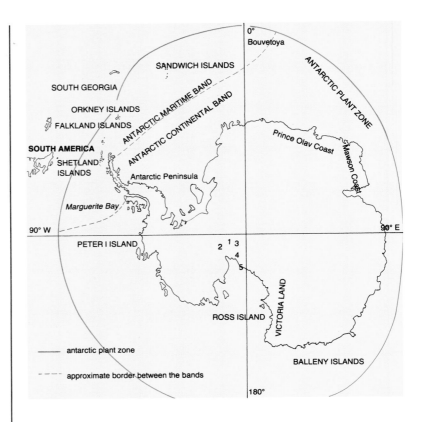

the extremes of winter cold. However, there is actually little water available for plants to absorb. This scarcity of water has a considerable influence on the soil's salt content. This represents another limiting factor, since more water would make the soil less salty.

Besides the latitude, the exposure of a given area to the sun is another determining factor for plant growth. The small portion of Antarctica that is ice free cannot be completely colonized by plant life because some parts of it are not well exposed to the sun. Vegetation is more regularly distributed on the large outcroppings and along the coasts. This is especially the case on the islands and on the Antarctic Peninsula. The nunataks, which are small, rocky reliefs emerging from the ice, are colonized by lichens. A lichen consists of an alga and a fungus living together. The alga provides food that is produced by the sun's energy, and the fungus gives the plant its water and its anchoring on the rocks.

Antarctic oases form in areas where the melting glaciers have exposed a large valley bottom. In these oases, the

Shown are lichens encrusted in the rocks of Signy Island in the South Orkneys. Lichens are a combination of an algae and a fungus. Despite their meager appearance, lichens produce a plant environment that is inhabited by several minute organisms.

temperature is considerably higher than on the surrounding glaciers. There is also a fair variety of life forms. The best known oases are the dry valleys of the transantarctic mountain chain across from Ross Island.

Most of the exposed land lacks vegetation. It has a barren appearance, similar to the landscapes of the moon and Mars. Only a few species of plants grow here. This greatly contrasts with the rich vegetation of other continents. There are only two species of flowering plants, eighty-five species of mosses, twenty-eight species of fungi, twenty-five species of liverworts, and about two hundred species of lichens. Of course, various species of algae are found in the marine environment.

The two species of flowering plants are found only on the Antarctic Peninsula. They are a hair grass and an herb, called "pink," that is closely related to the chickweeds. These two plants are also found at latitudes farther north. Other flowering plants have reached the Antarctic, but they have not succeeded in completely adapting. Most plants are not able to complete a full cycle, from flower to seed, in such a short season. This is the case with two species of spear grass and the creeping buttercup. The creeping buttercup produces infertile flowers and cannot reproduce.

Single-celled algae are pictured on the glacier of Signy Island in the South Orkneys. In the summer months, even the snow layer is colonized by these organisms. They form picturesque, thin blankets of red, green, or yellow colors.

Many species of mosses cannot grow in Antarctica, especially in the more continental areas. Several of the mosses grow on top of layers of dead moss. These layers can reach 6.5 feet (2 m) in thickness. The live mosses form only a small layer at the top, while the lower layers consist of dead mosses that have not decomposed. The age of these moss layers has been studied with radioactive carbon dating methods. These studies have revealed that some moss formations are five thousand years old, with an average annual growth of only 0.039 of an inch (1 millimeter).

A few species of liverworts grow among these formations. These flowerless, green plants are generally more delicate and require better conditions than the mosses. Their distribution is strictly limited to the coastal maritime zone.

Two species of gilled mushrooms are native to Antarctica. One of them, *Galerina antarctica*, grows among the clumps of hair grass. There are other types of nongilled fungi in the soil. The nonflowering plants cover only 3 to 4 percent of the exposed area. The flowering plants, however, do not exceed a covering of 0.001 percent. The distribution of the plants is greatly influenced by the soil types and the exposure to the sun.

Moving from the maritime to the continental band, the soil becomes more barren, and the vegetation seems to completely disappear. Here, lichens become the dominant plants, as they are the only ones adaptable to such extreme conditions. Even in the areas where the mosses cannot survive, one finds lichens that are inhabited by microscopic animals. The lichens provide shelter and food for these tiny organisms.

The tissues of the lichens are reduced in size as an adaptation to the environmental conditions. They are also of a dark color, which allows a better absorption of sunlight. A layer of threadlike fungus structures, or filaments, protects the algae's leaf tissues. This covering protects the plants from wind erosion and from losing too much water vapor through the leaf pores.

Beyond the areas where the lichens grow, a microscopic vegetation of bacteria and algae thrives between the cracks of rocks and on snowbanks. In the summer months, these single-celled algae create colored areas of red, green, and yellow on top of the snow.

These tiny communities are the most widespread life forms on the whole continent. Lichens and green and blue-

Several small invertebrate animals are typically found in the soil of the maritime and continental zones of Antarctica. *From top to bottom:* amoeba, nematode, tardigrade, and rotifer. The animals belonging to these four large groups are found almost everywhere on earth. They are very small and are visible only under a microscope.

green algae that are associated with bacteria form communities within the rocks. They live in the cracks as well as in between the relatively porous rock crystals, such as those found in granite or marble formations. As the cementing material between the rock crystals is dissolved by the living organisms, the rock is subject to a slow process of flaking away.

New species of plants are continually being transported by the wind from nearby continents. However, the new arrivals are not able to adapt immediately. Several species manage to survive for some time but do not succeed in reproducing. Even species of Antarctic plants do not reproduce successfully under the unusually harsh climatic conditions. In any case, the mosses and liverworts in Antarctica mainly reproduce vegetatively. That is, they reproduce by the growth of new tissue from already existing tissue.

All Antarctic plants have a notable capacity to survive for long periods in a frozen state while both dehydrated and inactive. They renew their life processes and growth as soon as conditions become more favorable. The plant species that do not have this capacity cannot survive into the next season. Scarce and scattered as it is, this vegetation is, nonetheless, the only food resource for a very specialized group of animals with surprising characteristics.

The Animals

In the Antarctic, all vertebrate animals depend on the resources of the ocean for their survival. Therefore, they must be considered a part of the marine environment. The land animals of Antarctica are essentially composed of invertebrates belonging to many different groups.

There are at least sixty-five species of protozoans, which are single-celled, microscopic animals. These animals are stable residents, at least on the Antarctic Peninsula. Some of them are ciliates, which have many hairlike extensions that look like eyelashes. Others are flagellates, which have one whiplike extension. Still other types are amoebas. Amoebas move about and capture food by means of temporary extensions of the cell body called "false feet." Some amoebas are bare, and some are protected by a microscopic shell. All protozoan species are found among mosses, and often on the bare ground.

Round, unsegmented worms called nematodes are also present in the Antarctic. They have colonized practically

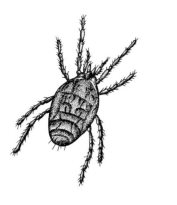

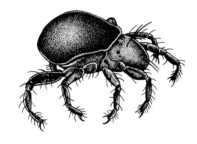

Pictured are more small invertebrate animals, typically found on land in the maritime and continental zones of Antarctica. All of these organisms are parasitic. *From top to bottom:* mite, tick, springtail, and midge. The first two are arachnids; the last two are insects.

every environment around the world. They even live inside the body of other animals as parasites. (A parasite is an organism that grows, feeds, and is sheltered on or in a different organism but does not contribute anything to the survival of its host.) Several species are parasites of birds and seals. There are at least seventy species of nematodes, some inhabiting land and some fresh water. They all show a high degree of specialization. Forty species are present in the maritime zone, including thirty-four native species.

On land, the nematodes reach a density of several million per square yard. In Antarctica, the total mass of their bodies in any given area is similar to that of the more temperate areas of the world (for example, Europe and the United States).

Along with nematodes, one can find tardigrades and rotifers, which are also called "water-bears." Tardigrades have short, plump bodies with stumpy legs and are closely related to insects, spiders, and crustaceans. They are less than 0.037 of an inch (1 mm) long. Although they have a delicate appearance, they are able to survive for long periods without water. This ability has enabled them to colonize the Antarctic environments. They live both in fresh water and on land. The rotifers have a mouth encircled by small hairs, a trunk, and a tapering foot region. They are also found in fresh water and on moist land.

The insects have difficulty in adapting to the Antarctic environment. With the exception of the forty-six species that are parasites of vertebrate animals, there are only twenty-one species of free-living insects. Most of them are wingless springtails, which measure from 0.037 to 0.074 of an inch (1 to 2 mm) in length. The springtail insects often gather in huge bunches made up of several tens of thousands of individuals. Two species of fungus gnats and a type of black fly called a "midge" are also found in the maritime zone. In the process of adapting to the cold, this midge species lost its capacity to fly because of a reduction in its wing size.

The number of insects is considerably larger in the subantarctic zone. Here one finds beetles, true bugs, wasps, and bees. Although spiders inhabit the subantarctic zone, they are not able to withstand actual antarctic conditions. However, their close relatives, the ticks and mites, are able to survive on the continent. These groups include several of the most resistant species known on earth. Many of these mites and ticks are parasitic. The free-living ones are char-

Illustrated are areas of distribution of the species and subspecies of mites (A) and springtail insects (B) on the subantarctic islands and on the Antarctic continent. For each zone, there is an indication of the total number of species (the numerator) as well as the number of native species (the denominator). The numbers along the lines with arrows indicate the number of species common to two different zones.

acterized either by a soft body or by a body protected by a sort of rigid shield.

Most of these invertebrates are mainly herbivores, which are plant-eaters, or debris-eaters. They play an important role in the environment. But there are also a few predators in this group. Most of these predators are mites that feed on other mites and springtails. One species of tardigrade and one species of nematode are also carnivores, or meat-eaters. In all though, the number of invertebrate predators in Antarctica is very small. This is particularly evident when one compares them to the numbers of available prey.

The food chain in this environment is quite simple, but the particulars of it remain unclear. Information on the life processes of several species has been gathered by only a few laboratories. None of the invertebrate species has been studied in its environment for a continuous year-long period. Therefore, the available data is incomplete and can be interpreted in different ways.

It appears that the animals are better adapted than the plants to survive the interior conditions of Antarctica. Mites and springtails are able to immediately colonize the interior nunataks. Single-celled algae and bacteria are the only plants that can survive in these areas. The animals' resistance to cold does not depend on their ability to survive the formation of ice in the body tissues, a situation that is rare in the animal world. Instead, it depends on their ability to

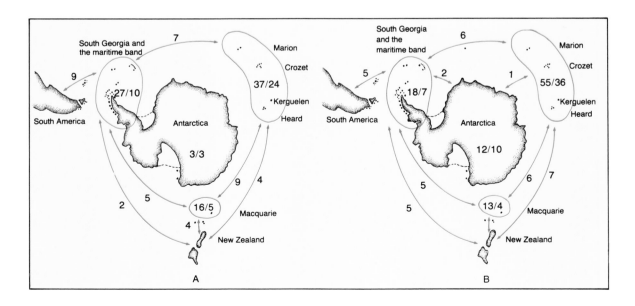

This rocky area on the Antarctic Peninsula is almost free of ice and snow.

accumulate substances that can act as an antifreeze. One such substance is the same chemical that is used as the basis for auto antifreeze. With this mechanism, many invertebrate animals can withstand body temperatures of -40° to -58°F (-40° to -50°C).

Each species has its own temperature limit, beyond which it cannot survive. These limits determine the distribution of the species in the Antarctic. The accumulation of antifreeze substances increases as the temperature drops. The larva of the black midge survives temperatures down to 5°F (-15°C), but it will perish at -4°F (-20°C).

Another cold-fighting mechanism used by the animals is to increase the rate of their body processes, or metabolism. In the Antarctic invertebrates, this rate is two to three times higher than in similar species of more temperate environments. Often, the small invertebrates remain trapped

This small frozen lake is found in the Antarctic Peninsula. Only a few very resistant organisms can survive in the nutrient-deficient lakes of the Antarctic. Their surfaces are covered by ice for over ten months of the year. Lakes with more nutrients are inhabited by more organisms, such as copepods and other crustaceans.

in the ice or in the cracks of the rocks. Since minute plants and other organisms that already live in these places use up all the available oxygen, these animals have adapted to long periods without oxygen. A study of the *Alaskozetes antarcticus* (mite) showed that 80 percent of its population was able to survive a 32°F (0°C) temperature, without oxygen, for a period of twenty-eight days.

Many species have evolved a flexible system of reproduction. They do not rely exclusively on a complete yearly cycle. Organisms that live in environments near the limit of

their survival capacity and that reproduce only once a year would be greatly harmed by an unfavorable season. Such an occurrence would prevent them from reproducing at all until the following year. Some animal species reproduce only once every two or three years. Other species reproduce many times in the same year. Because of this, during the same winter season one may encounter the same animal species in different stages of development. These adaptations increase an organisms chances of finding a favorable time for growth and reproduction.

With such a capacity for special adaptations, it would seem only natural that the Antarctic land animals would have evolved a large number of native species. However, many species arrived from neighboring lands. It is not clear exactly what the relationship is between the distances separating the various island groups and continents and the migrating species. Some species that appear to have no means of movement have been known to colonize new lands. For example, Bouvetoya Island originated from the ocean floor between 600,000 and 3 million years ago as a result of volcanic activity. Although it is about 1,056 miles (1,700 km) from the nearest island and over 1,243 miles (2,000 km) from the nearest continent (Africa), the island was colonized by three species of springtails and six species of ticks and mites.

Naturally, the closer the islands are to each other and to other land, the greater the number of species they have in common. The simplicity of the Antarctic animals represents an excellent example of this important concept of biogeography.

The combined effects of Antarctica's climatic conditions and its geographic isolation have produced a unique situation for its plant and animal communities. Their life forms have simple structures but complex features of specialization.

The Ecology of the Freshwater Lakes

Similar considerations are true for the ecology of the few freshwater pools found in this environment. Some of these lakes are oligotrophic. A body of water in this condition lacks plant nutrients and contains great amounts of dissolved oxygen.

There is also a variation in the salt content of some lakes. A layer of ice covers the surface of an Antarctic lake for many months. This layer isolates the lake from ex-

Glaciers, icebergs, mosses, and lichens
share Brialmont Cove near Cape
Spring, Graham Land.

changes with the external environment. Since the soils surrounding the lake are not fertile, the lake's surface waters do not contain nutrients. Often, there are not even enough nutrient substances available to fertilize the producing plants. Consequently, the lake remains poor in organisms and nutrients.

The lakes have different possible stages of development. They range from initial pools that form at the base of glaciers or in old glacial basins, to more mature lakes. The lakes near the coast may receive some salt from the sea or nutrients furnished by the colonies of birds and seals. The lakes with few nutrients are characterized by surfaces that are iced over for more than ten months of the year. They are inhabited only by a few species of algae, amoebas, nematodes, rotifers, and copepods.

The Ecology of the Saline Lakes

The conditions of saline lakes are different from those of the freshwater lakes. The saline lakes have two possible origins. Some are formed when, due to changes in the land formations, an arm of the sea becomes trapped in a fiord. After a period of evaporation, the water's salt content becomes more concentrated. Other saline lakes result from the accumulation of surface water, where the salinity has reached high levels from evaporation and sublimation. Sublimation is the changing of a solid to a gaseous state without first becoming a liquid, and vice versa.

When fresh water is added to these lakes from another source, different layers of water form. These layers have different levels of salinity and density. Various types of water layers occur in the lakes that form along the coast between the land and the ice. (These lakes originate from a closed-off arm of the sea.) In this case, the inflow of fresh water results in the formation of a surface layer of fresh water populated with the animals that typically inhabit these environments. Below this layer is a deeper layer of saline water, where marine animals are found.

Saline and freshwater lakes differ in their physical properties. In saline lakes, the salt concentration keeps the water from freezing at temperatures that are ten to twenty degrees below the freezing point of fresh water, which is 32°F (0°C). Under these conditions, the cold temperature would kill any animal in the water. However, in the freshwater lakes the insulation of the top layer of ice protects the water layers from sharp drops in temperature.

THE OCEAN ENVIRONMENT

Although Antarctica is a vast continent, the most spectacular features of its biology are associated with the oceans that surround it. If the Antarctic is considered part of the globe that lies within the line of the Antarctic Convergence, then it must be noted that over two-thirds of this region is occupied by ocean.

In a certain sense, the body of water some call the Antarctic Ocean is a unique ocean. In fact, the ice of certain areas of the ocean forms a continuity with the land of the continent. For many months of the year, the ocean is just an immense sheet of ice. Only in the summer, when it assumes a liquid appearance, does it resemble the rest of the world's oceans.

The presence of an ice crust changes the landscape of the ocean surface and greatly influences the life conditions. This is true both in the open waters and on the ocean bottom. During the summer, about 1.5 million sq. miles (4 million sq. km) of ice cover the ocean. This ice expands to about 8.5 million sq. miles (22 million sq. km) by winter. This dramatic seasonal change affects the life of the open waters.

The Action of Ice and Currents on the Biological Communities

All the Antarctic coasts undergo a series of mechanical disturbances unknown to other oceans. The ice that separates from the glaciers carries with it an enormous amount of rocks and rock fragments. These are deposited on the ocean floor in the form of sand and large pieces of stone. It has been estimated that about 500 million tons of material are carried away each year by this action. Enormous floating icebergs cut grooves across the sea bottom, upsetting the biological communities that live there. About 80 percent of an iceberg is under water. If the visible part is from 65 to 100 feet (20 to 30 m) high, the submerged part will come in contact with every area of the ocean bottom that is shallower than 328 to 492 feet (100 to 150 m) deep. Usually, ice forms only in the first 115 feet (35 m) of water. However, icebergs can often start the freezing process at the ocean bottom. The ice blocks that form there will then float to the surface, carrying with them the pieces of the ocean floor to which they were attached. This process further upsets the life of organisms living on the ocean bottom.

Nevertheless, with the exception of these mechanical disturbances, the bottom of the Antarctic Ocean has a stable

Opposite page: Two iceberg towers are connected under water in the Antarctic Ocean. The emerged part of an iceberg does not exceed 20 percent of the total mass. Thus, if an emerged part is 65 to 98 feet (20 to 30 m) high, the part under the water would be 328 to 492 feet (100 to 150 m) deep.

39

The Antarctic Covergence, which is indicated by the continuous line on the map, is a phenomenon of the Antarctic Ocean. It is a front where the cold water currents coming from the south meet the warmer currents coming from the north. The ocean is further influenced by other currents, the most important of which are the Weddell Current. *(indicated by the pink arrow)*, the western current *(indicated by blue arrows)*, and the eastern current *(indicated by green arrows)*. The western current moves in a clockwise direction, and the eastern current is nearest to the continent. The map also shows the limit of the main area of the ocean that is covered by ice *(indicated by the discontinuous line)* and the principal ice shelfs *(indicated by diagonal lines)*.

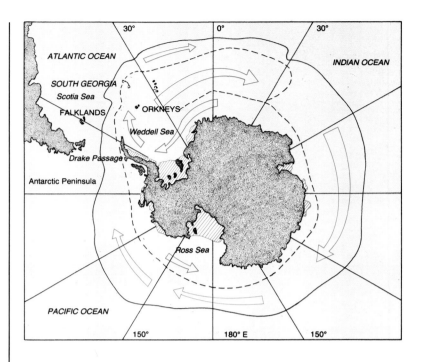

environment. Its temperature varies between 28° and 36°F (-2° and 2°C). This environment provides an enormous amount of living matter which serves as food for other organisms. A complex series of ocean currents circulates and mixes the waters of the Antarctic oceans. This process generates a continuous supply of nutrients.

The most important current in the Antarctic runs from west to east, between 40 and 60 degrees latitude south. Between this current and the Antarctic coast, another current moves from east to west. Furthermore, the colder and more dense Antarctic waters move toward the north. When they encounter the less dense, subtropical waters, they pass underneath.

The line where the two currents meet, as mentioned earlier, is the Antarctic Convergence. It is located between 54 and 62 degrees latitude south, varying according to the year and the geographic area. At the same time, a considerable movement of warmer water occurs in the deeper areas, just below the northward Antarctic Current. The warmer current moves in a southward direction, carrying waters that are rich in nutrients and salts. This current, referred to as the "deep circumpolar current," rises toward the surface when it reaches the coastal zones. At this point, the colder waters that originate along the coasts sink to the bottom.

The gigantic species of alga known as "kelp" is limited to the coasts of the subantarctic islands. It cannot withstand the extreme conditions off the coast of the Antarctic continent. These incredible algae reach a surprising length of 32 to 65 feet (10 to 20 m) and are capable of anchoring to the rocks by means of special tissues that resemble the roots of more evolved plants.

Once they reach the bottom, they begin to move north.

Unlike other continental shelves, the Antarctic continental shelf is not extensive, nor is it found at the usual depth of 656 feet (200 m). Because of the tremendous weight of the ice over the continent, the shelf is located at a depth of between 1,312 and 1,968 feet (400 and 600 m). Without the obstruction of a shallower shelf, the circulation of water is more complete near the coast.

The Antarctic Convergence is an important barrier for all the plant and animal species living in the open waters. These organisms are often found at different depths, according to the currents and the relative physical and chemical characteristics of the water. However, the Convergence does not affect the distribution of the bottom-dwelling animals.

The Ocean Bottom

The bottom-dwelling animal communities that live near the coasts are much different from those that are found farther away from the coasts. Near the coast, the bottom

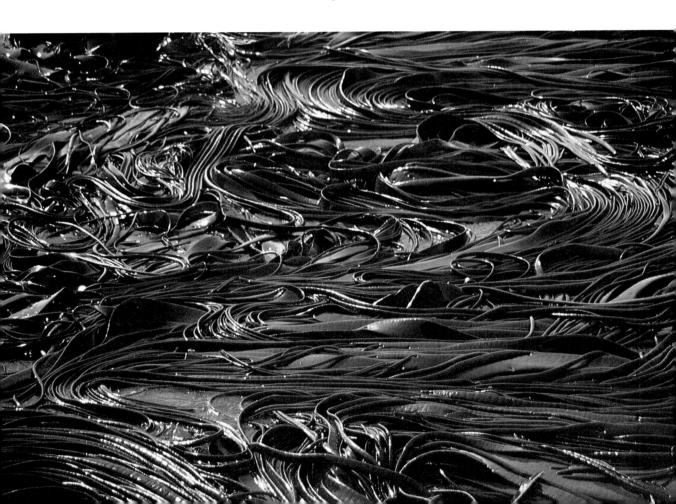

A 4-inch (10 cm) isopod crustacean crawls along the ocean floor. This is an excellent example of gigantism in the animals adapted to the extreme conditions of the Antarctic. This photograph was taken on the ocean floor off the Orkney Islands at a depth of 20 feet (6 m). This species is one of the largest isopods in the world. The large size decreases the animal's risk of freezing, which is an important factor in these waters.

dwellers are subject to the constant disturbing action caused by the movement of heavy ice blocks. In some areas of the ocean floor, this action has resulted in the so-called bare zones. These are found mainly around the islands and in rare sections along the rocky continental coast.

In the coastal regions, all the algae species are small, with some growing on rocks. The gigantic alga species known as "kelp" grows along the coasts of the subantarctic islands. This particular species cannot withstand the conditions of the higher latitudes.

The animals that live attached to the ocean bottom are rarely found in areas along the coasts. Otherwise, they would be easily swept away by the icebergs that fall into the water near the coasts. Animals with shells are more common. One of the better known species is the 2-inch (4-cm) limpet. Limpets are marine snails that cling to rocks. The limpet can withstand a temperature of -4°F (-20°C) for over two hours. During low tides, this animal covers itself with a layer of mucus as a protection against the sudden drops in air temperature. Another common marine animal is the chiton, which is also a shellfish that clings to rocks.

Amphipods, which are shrimplike crustaceans, and

This amphipod crustacean was photographed on the ocean floor near Signy Island in the Orkneys. Besides gigantism, the antarctic marine animals are characterized by the absence of larval forms and by a slow growth. The slow-growing antarctic organisms have a longer life span than organisms living in temperate zones.

rare clams are other bottom dwellers that live in this area. More common are the sea spiders and several species of ribbon worms. One species of ribbon worm is over 6 feet (2 m) long and is distributed throughout the Antarctic Ocean. In these waters, however, one does not find the classic acorn barnacles that are common along the coasts of more temperate areas. The gooseneck barnacles are the only barnacles that live on this ocean's bottom.

Seen from the coast, the Antarctic Ocean seems to be almost as barren as the region's land environments. Its true richness begins only several feet below the water surface, in areas where the organisms are more protected from freezing and from destruction by the ice. The algae are more numerous and luxuriant in deeper waters. Here, they contribute to form a complex environment where many animal species thrive.

The large perennial algae may grow from about 30 to 50 feet (10 to 15 m) long. They are not able to survive along coastal sections where the action of the ice is more destructive. They are normally found in the waters off coastal areas of exposed rock. Here they grow at depths of 110 to 130

Shown is a sea spider on the ocean floor near the Orkney Islands at a depth of about 82 feet (25 m). Sea spiders have eight legs like the true spiders, to which they are related. They eat mainly sea anemones, corals, hydroids, sponges, and marine moss animals. Sea spiders are present in the Arctic and the Antarctic, as well as in many tropical zones. They inhabit the deep waters and the open waters.

feet (35 to 40 m), although traces of vegetation have been found at even lower depths. The smaller algae, which grow from 3 to 6 feet (1 to 2 m) in length, appear under the branches of the larger species of red and green algae. Algae less than 3 feet (1 m) long are very numerous. They form a dense layer of vegetation.

Thousands upon thousands of amphipods are found among this vegetation. These shrimplike animals are the most numerous of the crustaceans and are represented by several species. They have colorings that camouflage them well on the ocean bottom. This is true of almost all bottom dwellers in this region. Few animals are brightly colored. These exceptions include an orange isopod crustacean, the brightly colored sea slugs, and the sea cucumber.

Many species of sea cucumbers, serpent stars, sponges, corals, and other organisms are typically found at the ocean bottom. However, the true shrimps, lobsters, and crabs are missing from these waters. This is surprising since they are found in almost every other ocean in the world. The part of the environment that they would normally inhabit is occupied by the beautiful, large isopod *Glyptonotus antarcticus*. This crustacean is found throughout the Antarctic Ocean. Another large isopod, *Serolis polita*, moves about on the ocean floor almost perfectly camouflaged.

Because of their great abundance, the sea spiders are perhaps the most noticeable animals. Three species have ten legs, and two species have twelve legs. They are found only in the Antarctic Ocean. As a whole, a large percentage of the antarctic bottom dwellers are native species. About 90 percent of the sea spider species and 50 percent of the sponges are native. The percentage of native species is 76 percent for the barnacles and 73 percent for the echinoderms (starfish, sea urchins, sea cucumbers, and sea lilies).

The bottom-dwelling animals have developed special adaptations to the physical characteristics of these waters and to the seasonal abundance of nutrients. There are at least three features that are unique to these animals, in comparison with their relatives of the temperate regions. These are slow growth (which results in a long life span), a large size (gigantism in many species), and the absence of larval forms living in the waters above the deep zone.

The slow growth is merely the result of an insufficient food supply. Thus, the animals have a longer life span than

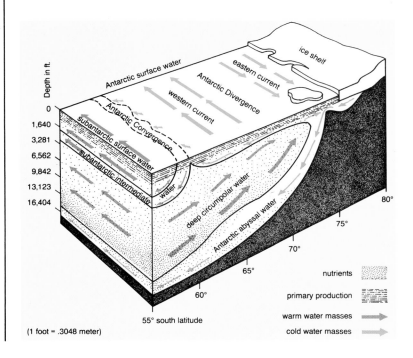

A high concentration of nutrients is brought to the surface by the rising of the warm circumpolar currents near the pole. This results in a rich growth of microscopic plants and a high availability of food for all of the other life forms. However, the production of the plants is limited by the roughness of the water. This turbulence prevents the algae from remaining at the ideal depth for harnessing the sun's energy.

Depth in ft.

0
1,640
3,281
6,562
9,842
13,123
16,404

Antarctic surface water
eastern current
ice shelf
Antarctic Divergence
western current
Antarctic Convergence
subantarctic surface water
subantarctic intermediate water
deep circumpolar water
Antarctic abyssal water

80°
75°
70°
65°
60°
55° south latitude

(1 foot = .3048 meter)

nutrients
primary production
warm water masses
cold water masses

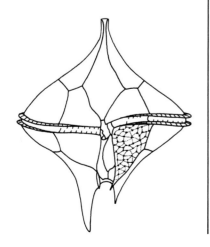

their relatives in temperate waters. It has been estimated that certain sea snails can live for over one hundred years. Another result of slow growth is gigantism, or abnormally large size. This occurs in many of the invertebrate animals, although not all invertebrates reach large sizes. It seems that the limited availability of calcium causes this abnormal development. This element is needed by several species for the growth of skeletal material.

The lack of a constant food supply partially accounts for the absence of larval forms in the upper water level. Because the algae "bloom" only in a certain season, a large number of larvae cannot survive in the upper water layers. Also, the low temperatures prevent a fast initial growth of the larvae.

To reproduce successfully, the invertebrate animals must use their available energy carefully. Their reproductive strategies include the production of fewer eggs. But these eggs have larger yolks. Thus, when the eggs hatch, the larvae are immediately independent and are not lost in the open waters. Animals that adopt this type of reproductive strategy are generally protective of their larvae during the first stages of development and growth.

In the Antarctic Ocean, only a few species of bottom-dwelling organisms have larvae that live in the upper water layers. They include two species of serpent stars, two species of sea stars, one species of sea cucumber, and one species of sea urchin. Almost all the invertebrate animals have developed different systems to protect their young. For instance, over 80 percent of the species of sponges do not deposit eggs but rather give birth to live larvae.

Plankton

The ocean floor environment is stable and limited in size. The environment of the plankton, on the other hand, is immense and associated with the interplay of various currents. These tiny, floating plants and animals have perhaps been studied more than any other biological aspect of the Antarctic. The plankton include the krill, which are small shrimplike crustaceans. Krill represent an immense natural resource that can be harvested for food. Because of the krill's potential economic importance, large investments have been made to learn about these organisms.

The first level of plankton production is represented by the growth of the phytoplankton, which are the plant members of the plankton community. The smallest of these

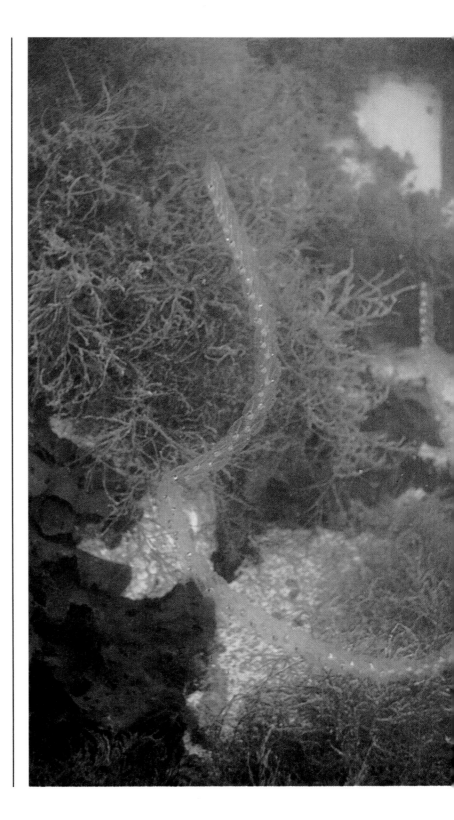

A chain of zooplankton called "colonial sea" squirts above an algae-covered area of the ocean bottom near Graham Land in Antarctica. It is made up of both microscopic animal species and larger species. There are many different groups of zooplankton in the Antarctic Ocean. Almost all their species are highly active and move about freely. The total mass of zooplankton produced in the Antarctic is much greater than that produced in the temperate or tropical seas.

are the microscopic algae called diatoms. Over one hundred species of diatoms have been described to date. Of these, only twenty are native to the Antarctic. Few species are common to both the Arctic and the Antarctic. Although the diatoms are the smallest element of the phytoplankton, they are nonetheless the most important. They produce organic material by photosynthesis. The diatoms determine the role that all the successive organisms will play in the food chain.

Throughout the cold season, these microscopic algae remain trapped in the ice of the ocean's top layer. As soon as the warmer weather thaws the ice, they begin to reproduce. The diatoms reach their maximum period of vegetative reproduction, or bloom, between spring and summer. In the higher latitudes, this occurs about one month later. These blooms are spectacular to see. Continuous bands or patches of color cover entire areas of the ocean and can be seen from great distances. The ocean water becomes more dense from the amazing numbers of diatoms that cover it for tens of thousands of square miles, often at depths of several yards.

The primary production of the Antarctic Ocean is almost all due to this seasonal phenomenon. Essentially, the production is high during this period of bloom. How-

A group of Adélie penguins swims near Graham Land. The penguins swim rapidly, leaping out of the water at frequent intervals. The numerous invertebrate animals are an important food source for many antarctic mammals and birds.

ever, its value becomes only average if it is spread out over the entire year. In this sense one could say that the Antarctic Ocean is no more productive than any other ocean.

The algal bloom is partially tied to the sudden availability of nutrients during the spring thaw. But more importantly, it is due to the renewed availability of solar energy. In this season the sun shines for longer periods, and it can penetrate beyond the water surface that is free of ice. The algal production, however, is not uniform throughout the Antarctic Ocean. Rather, there are striking differences between various zones. Not all of these differences can be explained in terms of currents and temperatures. In many cases, much research will have to be done to identify these different blooms. Basically, phytoplankton's reproduction is regulated by a complex mixture of factors that relate to the water's physical and chemical properties. Only the main aspects of these factors are known. The phytoplankton is numerous in comparison to the animals that feed on it. The animals do not seem to play an important role in controlling or limiting the algal bloom.

Phytoplankton is composed of more than just diatoms. Other organisms are abundant, such as the dinoflagellates, which are single-celled, photosynthetic organisms with two

The distribution of the various animal species around the Antarctic is determined by the location of the Antarctic Convergence and by the ice-covered surface of the ocean. It is also determined by the distribution of the krill. Since seals reproduce on the ice, their distribution follows the changing limit of the ocean ice. The map shows their distribution during the winter *(indicated by the broken blue line)* and during the summer *(indicated by the continuous blue line)*. The distribution of the seals that reproduce on the coasts of the subantarctic islands is indicated by red circles. The whale's distribution is shown by the continuous red line. The krill have moderately abundant concentrations *(indicated by the dotted zones)* and very abundant concentrations *(indicated by yellow zones)*. The most numerous colonies of penguins *(red dots)* and other marine birds correspond to the yellow zones. These birds feed on the krill.

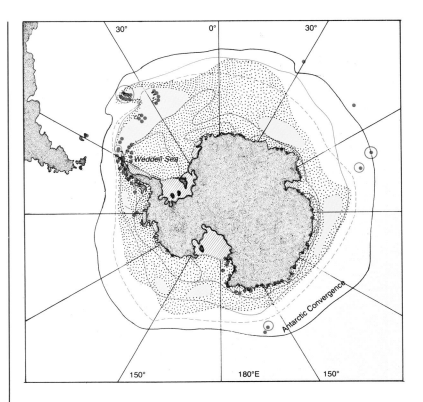

whiplike extensions. These organisms are difficult to collect and study, especially those that do not have a hard covering. Almost 80 percent of the dinoflagellates in the Antarctic are native, and most of the species belong to a single genus, *Protoperidinium*. Interestingly enough, the distribution of certain dinoflagellates of the genus *Ceratium* corresponds exactly to the location of the Antarctic Convergence. This group is found only north of this line.

Because they are so difficult to study, the dinoflagellates have probably been considered an unimportant part of the plant phytoplankton. But there is good evidence that suggests that this is not true. In several ocean areas, a large percentage of the total mass of living forms is made up of these organisms.

Other species of single-celled algae can occasionally become important and have blooms like those of the diatoms. One of these, *Dictyocha speculum*, is a good indicator of very cold waters, in which it is often more numerous than the diatoms.

Some scientists have theorized that phytoplankton contribute to the thawing of the ice in which they are trapped.

Its dark color supposedly increases the absorption of the sun.

It is certain that the greatest blooms and the maximum productivity occur in the coastal waters. The ice here is the last to thaw, but the coastal waters have a greater amount of plant nutrients. These nutrients rise from the richer layers of water that lie below the surface. Furthermore, the wind has less of an effect on the surface water. Thus, there is less mixing of the upper water layers. This enables the phyto-plankton to remain at the ideal water level for the absorp-tion of sunlight.

The irregular production of phytoplankton is the determining factor in the similarly irregular production of zooplankton. These are the animal members of the plank-ton community. Generally, the zooplankton is distributed throughout the Antarctic Ocean by the ocean currents. Zoo-plankton is composed of many species, but only a relatively small number make up the important mass populations.

Without a doubt, the most dominant organism is the krill. This is a sort of Antarctic shrimp that is the principal food of the large whales. It is most common in the waters south of the Antarctic Divergence. This is the line that separates the western current from the more interior eastern

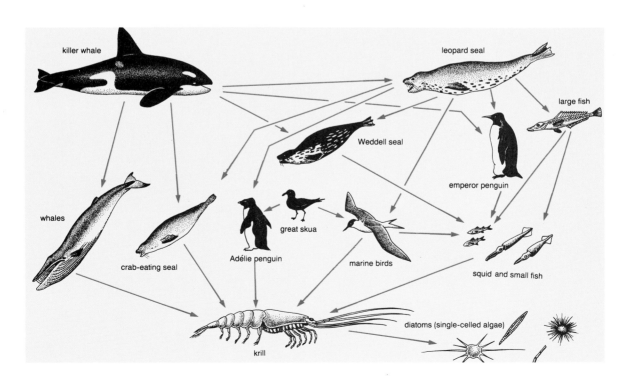

current. In the more external antarctic waters, zooplankton is composed primarily of copepod crustaceans. Three species of copepods make up 73 percent of the total mass of medium-sized plankton. (The krill is a small-sized plankton.)

Another unusual animal group is that of the arrowworms, which are second to the copepods in importance. The arrowworms have tapering, arrow-shaped bodies that are similar to those of roundworms. There are eighteen Antarctic species of arrowworms, all showing a limited tolerance for the water's different physical and chemical characteristics. Their distribution is a useful indicator of the various currents and other water movements.

Zooplankton migrate seasonally in a vertical direction. In the winter, they are found at depths of over 656 feet (200 m). In the summer, they are concentrated in the layer of the first 328 feet (100 m) of water. At this depth, the plant phytoplankton on which they feed are the most abundant. In the Antarctic, the total mass of zooplankton is much greater than in the temperate and tropical seas.

Krill

About half of the total mass of zooplankton is composed of the shrimplike krill, a name given to these organisms by Norwegian whalers. The largest and most common krill are almost 3 inches (7 cm) long. The species are concentrated in different areas of the ocean, some north of the Convergence and others along the continental shelf. Krill are particularly numerous near the islands of Orkney, Sandwich, and Shetland. Generally, most are found south of the Antarctic Divergence.

During the reproductive period, from January to March, the greatest concentrations of krill are found along the line of the Antarctic Divergence. The adult female deposits from two thousand to three thousand eggs at the water surface. The eggs sink down to a depth of about 2,460 feet (750 m) to the deep, warmer waters. During the next few years, as the hatched larvae gradually grow in size, they are found at shallower depths. Eventually they reach the water's upper level.

The adults live in enormous groups, sometimes at depths of 130 to 165 feet (40 to 50 m). These groups extend for hundreds of yards, if not hundreds of miles. In February 1981, the weight of one of these "schools" near Elephant Island was estimated at more than 2.5 million tons. Krill reach a concentration of thousands of individuals per cubic yard.

Opposite page: Several of the most common squid of the Antarctic Ocean are pictured. These animals are all quite small. The length of their bodies ranges from 2 to 12 inches (5 to 30 cm) not including the long, slender projections. However, in the Antarctic, there are also huge squid measuring from 3 to 13 feet (1 to 4 m).

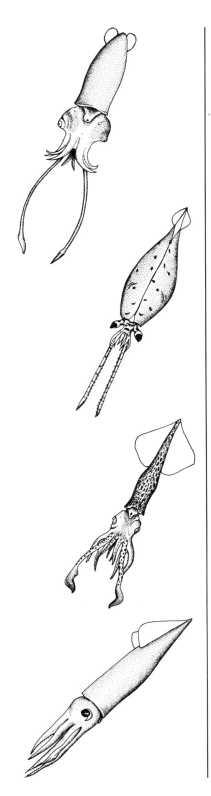

The reason for their gathering is not known. The adults all swim with their heads facing in the same direction, moving parallel to each other. They signal their positions in the water by flashes of light made by particular organs scattered throughout their bodies. The eyes of the krill are adapted to perceive this light. They have a high content of vitamin A, which aids sight.

The connection between the krill and the organic production of phytoplankton is important. Both groups have an effect on the other. After feeding on phytoplankton, the krill release a large part of the nitrogen contained in the plankton back into the ocean. The nitrogen is expelled in a form that can be readily utilized by the various plants. In other words, the krill fertilize their own food.

Since much less food is available in the winter, the krill lose a considerable amount of weight during that period. Their growth is thus postponed until the summer period. The krill seem to have a long life span. They live at least forty years and reproduce up to two times per year for one to three years.

Because of their biological characteristics, the krill represent the central element of all the environments of the Antarctic seas. Their enormous concentrations form the basic food source of all other living organisms in Antarctica. These include mollusks (shellfish), fish, birds, seals, and whales. The krill are especially important to the whale's diet. Because of the gathering behavior of the krill, whales are able to feed on them easily. They simply swim among the krill with their mouths open.

Even humans have begun to take a closer look at this food resource. A new fishing technology has enabled the gathering and processing of large quantities of krill all on the same boat. Presently, an increased amount of krill can be caught and made available to the human food industry. This surplus is due to the large decline in the whale populations.

A fishing boat with suitable nets can easily catch ten to fifteen tons of krill in an hour. This is an enormous catch in such a short time. Russian krill fishers immediately sort the krill according to length and press them to extract the soluble protein. This protein is later thickened with heat to form a sort of paste. In contrast, the Japanese immediately package the krill as a product for the market. A large part of the catch is used as a fertilizer or to feed livestock. This, however, does not seem to be an efficient use of such an

An antarctic cod is a typical fish of the Antarctic Ocean. A rather high percentage of the fish species in these waters is native. This situation is the result of few exchanges with the neighboring fish of the temperate oceans.

important food resource.

The stock of krill now available has been estimated at between 125 million and 5 billion tons. A more conservative estimate would be range between 500 and 700 million tons. The annual production of krill is estimated between 750 million and 1.3 billion tons. If one considers that the total weight of fish caught in the world is about 70 million tons, it is easy to understand why krill is seen as an excellent food resource for humans. Its availability is practically unlimited.

However, the main consumers of krill are the large whales. Since the whale populations have been greatly reduced in recent years, larger amounts of krill are now available. But today, many groups are fighting to protect the whales. It is thus possible that the availability of krill will decrease in the future if the whales increase in number.

The study of krill is an important aspect of research programs in the Antarctic. Information on their reproductive biology, life processes, and movements is still limited. Furthermore, it is necessary to find more reliable methods of estimating the krill populations and managing their harvest to take full advantage of their potential value to

humans in an era of world hunger.

Octopuses and Squid

The octopuses and squid make up another group of invertebrates that play an important role in the Antarctic's food chain. This group also includes the cuttlefish as well as the giant octopus. The medium- and large-sized ocean squid are particularly important. They prey on the krill and, in turn, are preyed upon by such carnivores as seals and whales.

Not all scientists agree on the importance of this invertebrate group, since the available information is small and conflicting. Nets with an opening of about 10 sq. yards (9 sq. m) are used in the research studies carried out in the Antarctic Ocean. Until recently, only a few squid and octopuses were caught, and almost all of them were small. Therefore, a sampling of the entire group of these animals was not available.

However, the analysis of the stomach content of many seals and large marine birds revealed that there is a large number of octopuses and squid in the upper levels of the food chain. In the stomach of one sperm whale, for example,

Another characteristic antarctic fish was photographed near Signy Island in the Orkneys.

the remains of over eighteen thousand squid were found. These remains consisted primarily of the horny parts of the squid's mouths. These horny parts enable the squid to cut off even the most resistant scales and shells of the invertebrate animals upon which they prey.

When the fishing industry began to use larger nets in Antarctic Ocean waters, larger species of squid were caught. It was then concluded that the accuracy of sampling the squid and octopuses in the open sea is closely tied to the efficiency of the fishing instruments used. Small nets are not adequate to provide a true picture of the various populations that inhabit these waters.

To date, about twenty species of squid have been identified. They range in size from 3 to 13 feet (1 to 4 m), not counting the animal's long, slender projections known as "tentacles." Little is known of their biology. Several species grow slowly. Others reproduce only at depths of over 3,280 feet (1,000 m). Still others reach sexual maturity at only one or two years of age. Several species have very long tentacles with thousands of small suction cups. The majority of the species have light-producing organs that are located in

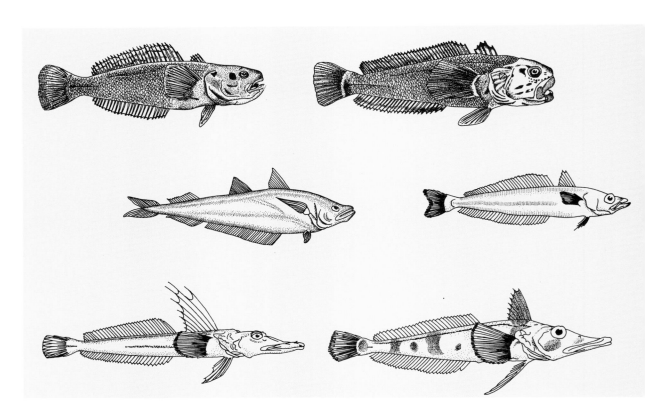

different parts of their bodies. The squid uses these lights to attract prey, to communicate its position to other members of the same species, and to evade predators.

The squid is able to change the intensity of the light in the organs located on the lower side of its body. The light from its underside blends with the sunlight that filters through the water. The intensity of the light produced varies according to the depth at which the animal is found at any given moment. Because of this mechanism, a predator swimming below the squid is not able to distinguish its outline against the water surface.

Given their size, it would seem that squid and octopuses have some influence on the populations of krill and fish upon which they feed. Octopuses and squid, in turn, are eaten by a large number of predators.

But the attempt to measure the predator influence is made difficult by the variety of potential predators, such as penguins, sperm whales, and albatrosses. Nevertheless, one can calculate that about thirty to thirty-five million tons of squid and octopuses are eaten every year. On the other hand, squid and octopuses probably eat about one hundred

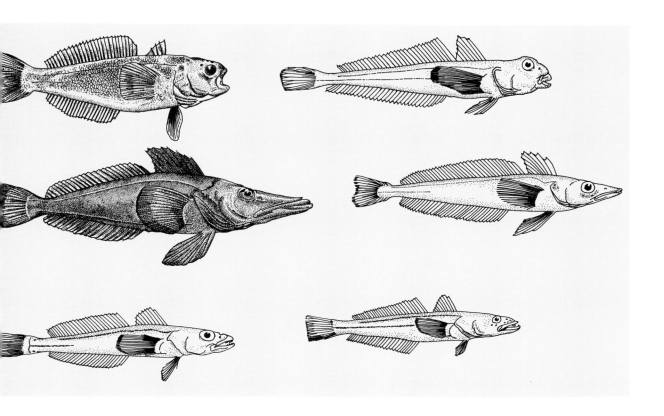

million tons of krill per year. They make seasonal and daily migrations in order to follow their food sources.

Further research on the energy cycles of the Antarctic Ocean environments should include a more thorough study of squid and octopuses. It is hoped that new and more effective techniques can be developed for this research.

Fish

Only a limited variety of fish inhabits the waters of the Antarctic Ocean. The antarctic fish number about two hundred species, belonging to thirty different families. This represents about 1 percent of all the fish species on earth. About 60 percent of these two hundred species and about 90 percent of the entire fish population of Antarctica belong to just four families. The members of these families have a great variety of forms. Because of this, they are able to occupy different niches of the environment. (A niche is an area within an environment that supplies an organism with all it needs to survive.)

Most species of Antarctic fish are bottom dwellers, living near the coast. However, since the continental shelf of Antarctica is located at a depth of from 1,640 to 2,460 feet (500 to 750 m), these fish have many of the features that are typical of deep-water organisms. Over 85 percent of the species are native to these waters, but their distribution is not the same throughout the Antarctic Ocean.

The open-sea fish, on the other hand, exhibit a lower percentage of native species. Only about 25 percent of these open-sea species are native to Antarctica. This is because these species can come in contact with and mate with similar species that live in the nearby temperate oceans. Therefore, a lot of crossbreeding occurs which limits the numbers of native Antarctic offspring.

Antarctic fish never reach large sizes. Apart from a few exceptions, it is rare that they exceed 16 inches (40 cm) in length. The antarctic fish have a series of interesting adaptations. The mechanism of resistance to cold is probably one of the most important of these. The freezing point of the blood of marine fish around the world (with the exception of the primitive species) is 31°F (-0.5°C). The average annual temperature in the antarctic waters is considerably lower than this. Therefore, the fish in the Antarctic had to evolve mechanisms to combat the cold.

Under extremely cold conditions, several fish species have learned to avoid coming into contact with ice crystals,

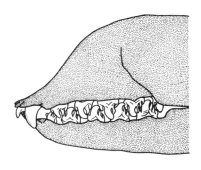

The teeth of the crab-eating seal are unusual. The lobes of the teeth of the upper jaw fit perfectly into the spaces between the lobes of lower teeth. The teeth form a sort of large sieve. They are used by the animal to filter the krill from the water. Despite its name, the crab-eating seal does not feed on crabs. Its primary food source is krill. It is not known whether the seal captures the krill one by one or whether it captures a group of krill in one mouthful. The first method is the most probable.

A Weddell seal comes up to breathe through a hole cut in the ice. This seal can reach a length of 10 feet (3 m) and a weight of 882 to 1,102 pounds (400 to 500 kg). The Weddell seal is found in coastal environments and is one of the most numerous seals of its family. Its total population has been estimated at about one million.

which would begin an unstoppable process of freezing. Other species have evolved a system of circulating a chemical antifreeze in their bodies. This substance lowers the freezing point of the fish to 28°F (-2°C). All fish that have the ability to produce antifreeze are also characterized by kidneys that retain this precious chemical within the body.

Many of the so-called white-blooded fish species have another adaptation. Their blood contains few red blood cells, which normally carry oxygen in all other fish (and all vertebrate animals). In the white-blooded fish, however, oxygen is transported by the clear fluid portion of the blood called "plasma." These fish have many tiny blood vessels in the skin and fins that are used to extract oxygen from the water. They also have a higher heart output and a higher rate of blood flow than other fish. With these adaptations, the white-blooded fish can move about in the cold waters just as easily as any red-blooded species.

Many bottom-dwelling species of fish do not have a swim bladder. A swim bladder is a gas-filled sac that helps the fish float. As a result, they are unbalanced and cannot float at different depths. Since they are heavier than the water, they tend to sink to the ocean floor. Generally, they

A leopard seal swims under water near the Orkney Islands. This powerful animal preys on many large vertebrates that live in the same environment. These include other species of seals and penguins. The leopard seal can be considered a superpredator. In the food chain, it is found just below the killer whale.

remain there.

The water near the surface is rich, however, with krill, an important food resource for the fishes' food chain. Several fish species make regular vertical migrations to feed on the krill. They have developed certain features that help them reach the surface even though they lack a swim bladder. Some species, for example, have lighter skeletons made of fibrous tissue, or cartilage, rather than heavier bones. Others have large deposits of fat that make them more buoyant.

Generally, antarctic fish have a slow growth and do not reach maturity for several years after birth. They often spend their first years near the coasts, venturing into more open waters only to feed on krill.

The young of some species occasionally make seasonal migrations. The giant antarctic cod is an example of a migratory fish, and because of its migrations, this species is easily caught by fishermen. Since there are no restrictions on the size of nets and mesh that can be used by fishermen, many young fish are captured before reaching sexual maturity. If too many young are caught, the species will not be able to maintain its population level, since not enough

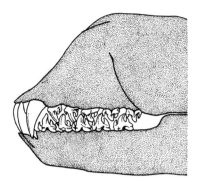

The leopard seal has four canine teeth, which are used to tear apart large prey. The remaining teeth have pointed lobes. Like the crab-eating seal, the lobes of the upper teeth fit perfectly into the spaces between the lobes of the lower teeth. This set of teeth enables the leopard seal to eat a wide variety of animals including krill, small fish, and even large vertebrate prey.

young will reach the breeding age. Therefore, prolonged and excessive fishing activity can be damaging to most species.

There are examples of good fishing years in which thousands of tons of fish have been caught. These were then followed by years of rapid decline. Today, accurate studies on the growth cycles of these fish are urgently needed. It is important that researchers learn to determine the age and reproductive state of a fish by its size. With better information available, there are more chances of saving certain species from overfishing. However, it may already be too late for some species.

Since antarctic fish feed primarily on krill, researchers have tried to estimate the impact the fish have on the krill populations. It seems that the fish eat about 50 to 100 million tons of krill each year. Two fish species, *Notothenia rossii* and *Champsocephalus gunnari*, eat more krill than any other species. By comparison, the amount of fish eaten by seals and marine birds has been estimated at about 15 million tons per year.

Seals

Seals are mammals that have been successful in adapting to the antarctic environment. The true antarctic seals descended from an evolutionary branch of seals of the more temperate areas, the monk seals. They arrived in the Antarctic between 10 and 15 million years ago. They then evolved into four different species—the crab-eating seal, the Weddell seal, the Ross seal, and the leopard seal.

Two other species, the elephant seal and the Kerguelen fur seal, also arrived in the southern ocean. However, they did not develop radical adaptations to the new environment, and have remained more closely tied to semitemperate environments. These last two species differ from the more typically antarctic seals. For example, they are able to live together in the same environment without violent conflicts over food and living space.

The most visible species is that of the crab-eating seal, perhaps one of the most common large mammals in the world. The total mass of all crab-eating seals put together is about four times that of all the other flippered animals on earth. Their numbers have been estimated at between 15 and 20 million animals. Crab-eating seals are large. The female is about 6 feet (2 m) long and weighs 506 pounds (230 kilograms), while the male is slightly smaller. The

A crab-eating seal swims beneath the ice. It has been estimated that each year the antarctic seals eat about 130 million tons of krill, 10 million tons of squid and octopuses, and 8 million tons of fish.

brown coat is speckled with dark spots that contrast with the light background. The spots are particularly numerous on the sides, behind the front flippers. The coats of the crab-eating seals are often cut and scarred in various places, the result of attacks by leopard seals and killer whales.

Living in the more open waters on the outermost part of the ice pack, crab-eating seals rarely go near the coasts or the permanent ice. Because they are so numerous, it is not uncommon to see individuals scattered in distant areas, such as the subantarctic waters.

The mouth of the crab-eating seal is highly specialized. The teeth have a complex shape and are used to filter krill from the water. Each tooth has several different size lobes. Those of the upper teeth fit perfectly between those of the lower teeth. The name "crab-eating" is inappropriate as these animals do not feed on crabs. Over 90 percent of the

diet of this animal is composed of krill. The remaining 10 percent is made up of fish, squid, and octopuses. It is estimated that the crab-eating seals eat about 63 million tons of krill per year.

The Weddell seal is larger than the crab-eating seal. The female is about 10 feet (3 m) long and weighs between 880 and 1,100 pounds (400 to 500 kg). The male is a bit smaller. This seal is characterized by a short snout and a stocky appearance. Its coat is blue-gray with numerous spots. The newborn are dark brown in color.

This species is very large. An accurate count of its population is difficult because it frequents zones that are hard to access. Nevertheless, the total population has been estimated at between 800,000 and 1,000,000.

The Weddell seal lives near the coast and even inhabits areas where the ice thaws for only a few months of the year. In these zones, the seal makes a hole in the ice with its teeth and keeps it free of any accumulation of snow or ice. Because it is commonly found on the coast, this species is the best known to those who visit the Antarctic. It is also relatively tolerant of the presence of humans. The Weddell seal feeds primarily on fish (53 percent), octopuses and squid (11 percent), and other invertebrate animals (36 percent). This seal can swim in deep water for long periods of time while fishing for its favorite prey, the giant antarctic cod, in waters of medium depth.

The Ross seal is not as well known. This is due to its limited population and its preference for the more interior zones of the ice pack. (These zones are not visited as much by researchers.) The Ross seal is also the smallest of seals, having a length of about 6 feet (2 m) and a weight that rarely exceeds 440 pounds (200 kg). Like the other species, the male is slightly smaller than the female.

This species can be easily recognized because of its short snout and large eyes. It also has a unique striped pattern along the body, beginning at the corner of the mouth. The hind flippers are longer in comparison to the rest of the body. Its population, numbering an estimated 230,000 animals, is unevenly distributed. The diet of the Ross seal consists of octopuses, squid, fish, krill, and other invertebrate animals.

The leopard seal is one of the largest seals. The female has an average length of about 10 feet (3 m) and an average weight of 816 pounds (370 kg). Some leopard seals have been known to weigh as much as 1,102 pounds (500 kg). It is

a powerful animal with strong teeth. The long, tapered body and flattened head are features that contribute to its great swimming speed. The leopard seal is an eager predator, feeding on anything within its reach. Nevertheless, it still has certain food preferences. Its diet consists of large vertebrates, such as penguins and other seals, fish, squid, octopuses, krill, and other invertebrate animals.

The crab-eating seal is one of the leopard seal's favorite prey. Younger crab-eating seals are more often captured since they are not as skillful as the adults in fleeing. The leopard seal has also long been considered to be a great predator of penguins. It gets this reputation from observations made in areas where the penguins leave and enter the water. Only the young penguins are easy prey, however. The adults are able to escape by swimming rapidly and confusing the leopard seals.

The name of this seal species does not derive exclusively from its predatory habits. It also comes from the coloring of its coat. Its back is dark gray with light spots, while its underside is silvery with dark spots.

Unlike most other species, leopard seals are distributed over a large area. They are found from the coast all the way to the subantarctic islands, although their population density is low. The total population of this species has been estimated at about 220,000 individuals. The leopard seal is a solitary animal. Rarely is it seen in small groups. Even in these situations, there does not seem to be any type of social ties among the group's individuals.

Next to the whales, the elephant seal is one of the largest marine mammals. A large male can weigh up to 5 tons and exceed 16 feet (5 m) in length. The female is always much smaller, generally not larger than 10 feet (3 m) in length and one ton in weight. The fur is short, and the coat has a uniform coloration somewhere between gray and light brown. The young, on the other hand, are born completely black. They become iron gray after four weeks, at the end of the first molting. Molting is the process by which an animal sheds its old hair for a growth of new hair.

Although they are distributed throughout the southern ocean, elephant seals are actually found more often in three large concentrations. These are located in the area of the islands near the Convergence, around South Georgia, around Kerguelen and Heard, and around Macquarie. They do not like ice and are rarely seen on the ice pack. Their total population is estimated at around 800,000 animals,

Several large whales are found in the Antarctic Ocean. The left side of the illustration shows *(from top to bottom)* the blue whale, the finback whale, the Sei whale, and the Minke whale. The right page of the illustration shows *(from top to bottom)* the southern rorqual whale, the humpback whale, the killer whale, and the sperm whale. These last two species, which are toothed whales, do not feed on krill. The killer whale hunts large vertebrate prey, while the sperm whale preys on gigantic squid.

although this figure may be inaccurate.

The elephant seal is a powerful, heavy animal that moves with great difficulty on the land, although it is very agile in the water. The layer of fat under the skin protects it from the cold. Its physical structure enables it to swim to great depths. Seventy-five percent of this animal's diet consists mainly of squid and octopuses. Fish account for the remaining 25 percent.

Another interesting species is the Kerguelen fur seal. The once immense populations of Kerguelen seals on the subantarctic islands had been almost completely wiped out by the middle of the nineteenth century. Thanks to protective measures and changing tastes in the fur industry, these seals have made a comeback in recent decades. Today, their population is estimated at about one million animals. It is hoped that this species will reach its original number of

several million by the end of the century.

The male Kerguelen fur seal is much larger than the female, reaching a length of 6 feet (2 m) and a weight of from 330 to 440 pounds (150 to 200 kg). The female is less than 4 feet (1.4 m) long and weighs under 110 pounds (50 kg). The fur of this species is different from that of most other seals. In the Kerguelen seal, an outer layer of fur covers the underfur. This helps to insulate the body from the cold, since these animals lack a substantial layer of fat under the skin. The male is also characterized by a sort of mane that makes it seem larger.

At least 80 percent of this seal's diet consists of krill. The remaining 20 percent is made up of fish, squid, and octopuses. The Kerguelen fur seal lives in the open water for almost all of the year, except during the breeding period. It is seldom found in the waters of the ice pack or on the coast.

A humpback whale makes a spectacular leap out of the water. These unique exhibitions are probably used as a communication device among whales of the same species.

If one considers the distribution patterns and food habits of the various seals, it is easy to see why there is no direct competition among them. In fact, one species is a wide-ranging predator while the others have notable food specializations.

Whales

Whales are very mobile and can move through all of the oceans of the world. Many species are found in both the arctic and antarctic waters. Many other species make long migrations from the polar to the temperate and tropical regions. In the Antarctic, there are six species of baleen whales. Baleen whales make up one of two groups into which whales are divided. Unlike the other group, the toothed whales, the baleen whales have no teeth. Instead, these whales have fringed plates, called "baleen," which they use to filter small marine organisms out of the seawater. In the Antarctic, there also are several species of toothed whales.

The six baleens are the blue whale, the finback whale, the Sei whale, the Minke whale, the southern rorqual, and the humpback whale. The blue whale is perhaps the largest mammal that has ever existed on earth. It can reach a length of 98 feet (30 m) and a weight of 150 tons.

The sperm whale is the largest of the toothed whales. The male of this species reaches a length of 59 feet (18 m) and a weight of 70 tons, while the female does not exceed 36 feet (11 m) in length and 17 tons. The sperm whale has only one blowhole, while many other whales have a double blowhole.

The killer whale is another toothed whale that is common in the Antarctic. It does not exceed 26 to 30 feet (8 to 9 m) in length and it weighs between seven and eight tons. The female is generally smaller than the male.

Unlike their relatives of the arctic waters, the antarctic whales do not have a large number of species. However, before they were extensively hunted, the total mass of the antarctic whales was five times greater than that of the arctic whales.

Whales have been hunted in the Antarctic since the first years of the nineteenth century. With the invention of the harpoon-launching cannon in 1864 and the founding of hunting stations on land in 1904, the whalers began to kill incredible numbers of animals. In 1904, a total of 195 whales were hunted by the only existing hunting station on

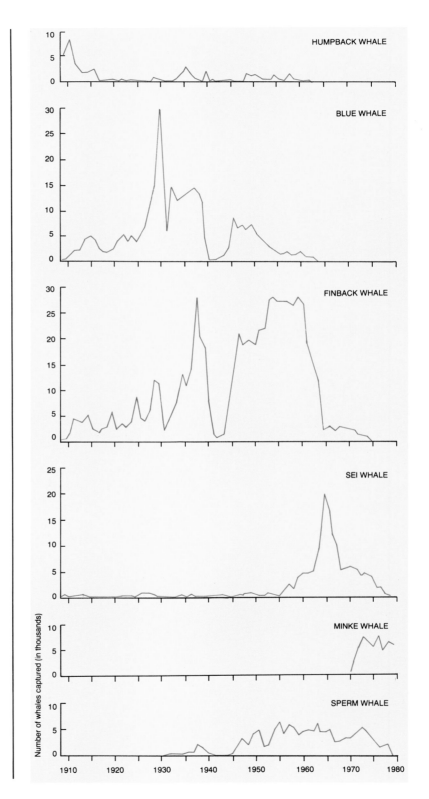

This series of graphs shows the trend of the annual capture (by whalers) of six whale species in the Antarctic from 1910 to 1980. *From top to bottom:* humpback whale, blue whale, finback whale, Sei whale, Minke whale, and sperm whale. In practically all cases, after a progressive increase in the numbers captured, there was a large drop in the numbers captured. This was due to the nearly total exhaustion of the whale populations.

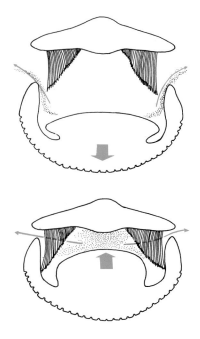

This drawing illustrates the feeding method of a baleen whale. Above, the whale opens its mouth, which fills with water and food substances. The whale then brings its tongue up against the roof of its mouth, forcing the water out and trapping the food among the baleens.

land. In 1913, 10,760 whales were hunted by 6 stations, using 21 processing boats and 62 hunting boats.

Later, the whalers began to use boats that were large enough to handle all the processing work on board, without having to rely on land bases. When this change took place, the number of whales killed suddenly rose to forty thousand per year. Despite the interruption of the war years, this massacre continued until the 1950s. By then, the era of the whaler was over, due to the extremely low populations of whales. The blue whale had become the rarest species.

The sperm whale has almost always been spared from large-scale hunting because of the inferior quality of the oil that can be produced from its fat. The processing of this oil involves the use of many different containers and methods. The killer whale has also been spared from extensive hunting because the value of the products that are derived from this animal are not worth the efforts to hunt it.

Presently, only Japan and the Soviet Union continue to hunt whales. They capture between seven thousand and eight thousand Minke whales per year. Provided that all countries agree to support the restriction, all whale hunting will be outlawed within a few years. However, protests have already been voiced over this restriction. Before the great massacres, the number of whales was estimated at about 1.1 million animals. These had a total mass of about 45 million tons. More than a million whales ate about 190 million tons of krill, 14 million tons of squid and octopuses, and 5 million tons of fish per year. Given these large figures, one would assume that there was a certain competition for food among the whales. The extensive consumption of krill by the whales must also have affected other animals that feed on these organisms.

Today, the total mass of the whales is estimated at only 9 million tons. Their annual food consumption is calculated at about 43 million tons of krill, 6 million tons of squid and octopuses, and 130,000 tons of fish. It would thus seem that a great surplus of krill is now available, and the fishing industry is already looking into the possibility of harvesting this surplus.

BIRDS

People think that many different bird species live in Antarctica. This notion, which is not altogether true, is based on the reports of the first expeditions to the area. Most of these expeditions took place in summer, especially along the most accessible coastal areas and on the subantarctic islands. These areas are the preferred nesting areas of many bird species that gather there in large numbers. However, many of these species completely abandon the Antarctic region in the winter, or they scatter out into the open sea. In Antarctica, the average bird density is always lower than the bird density of temperate areas. In winter, this density drops to extremely low levels.

The most striking concentrations of birds are those of the nesting penguins. They are certainly among the most fascinating specimens of the animal kingdom. The penguins alone account for more than 90 percent of the total mass of antarctic birds. There are only seven species of penguins, and the remaining bird communities of the Antarctic are made up of a few species belonging to two main orders. The first, the order Procellariiformes, is comprised of the albatrosses, petrels, shearwaters, and fulmars. The second order, Charadriiformes, is that of the gulls, terns, skuas, jaegers, and sheathbills. The total number of species amounts to only about fifty. Six species of albatrosses and twenty-three petrels make up the majority of these.

Penguins

Penguins have almost become the symbol of Antarctica. This is not entirely due to their unique shape and the ease with which they can be approached and observed. A large element in this symbolism is the fact that they are almost exclusive to this region. All eighteen living species of penguins are distributed in the Southern Hemisphere. The two largest species live in the Antarctic, as well as five medium-sized species. The smallest of the antarctic penguins, the rockhopper penguin, is also the smallest warm-blooded animal of this polar region. It weighs only 5 pounds (2.5 kg). The largest species, the emperor penguin, weighs 66 pounds (30 kg).

Generally, the penguins have developed adaptations to the environmental conditions of the Antarctic that are more effective than those of many other species. These adaptations are certainly striking at first sight. Fossil evidence shows that up to three million years ago, the penguins evolved primarily in temperate waters. Since then, these

Opposite page: A sooty albatross sits on its nest on South Georgia. Marine birds are numerous in the Antarctic due to the large numbers of fish, squid, and crustaceans on which they feed.

Gentoo penguins are found over a vast area that ranges from Tierra del Fuego and the Falkland Islands to the Shetland and Orkney islands. South Georgia and other subantarctic islands are also inhabited by this species. The gentoo is one of the largest species of penguins. It measures about 30 inches (76 cm) in length. The king and emperor penguins are the only other large penguins.

animals have managed to develop structural and functional features that help them to withstand the harsh polar conditions.

The most evident characteristics of this evolution are the spindle-shaped body, strong muscles for swimming, and wings that have been transformed into flippers. A thick layer of fat under the skin and an additional layer of special feathers protect the penguins from the cold. Unlike other birds, the feathers completely cover every part of the body with a uniform density. Each feather is short with a wide, flattened quill. Small threads of down branch off from the quill, overlapping with the downy threads of the other feathers. The result is an efficient covering. By lowering or raising its feathers, the penguin can control the amount of insulation.

Out of water, over 80 percent of the penguin's insulation is due to the feathers. However, in the water it is the fat layer that protects the animal against the cold. The largest penguins have a fat layer almost 1 inch (2 cm) thick. The fat deposit varies according to the season and the temperature. It also varies according to the periods during which the penguin relies on it for energy. The penguin has an extensive system of blood vessels that can efficiently transport the fat. The animal can increase or decrease the flow of

A colony of king penguins is spotted on South Georgia. In the foreground are numerous plump young penguins covered by thick, grayish brown down. The larger species of penguins inhabit the coldest zones of Antarctica. This shows that in the coldest climates the tendency to gigantism increases an animal's advantage. The higher ratio of body volume to surface area helps to conserve body heat.

blood and, thus, control the transport of fat in relation to the atmospheric temperature.

Actually, the greatest problem for animals that are so well equipped to live in cold environments is the danger of overheating when they are on land. In the summer, the sun can become quite warm. Many species breath rapidly in order to release excess heat from their body, and occasionally, they even eat snow to keep cool. The blood flow to the flippers can also be regulated. When the animal is too hot, there is more blood flow to the flippers, which give off excess heat. The two largest species, the emperor penguin and the king penguin, run the greatest risk of becoming overheated. Since movement increases body heat, the king penguin immediately starts to breathe rapidly anytime it moves onto the land. The emperor penguin, instead, simply refuses to move. In this way, it does not generate any excess heat. Colonies of emperors are the most peaceful and quiet of all the penguin colonies. The strong, cold polar wind does not affect this penguin's body temperature because the insulation of its feathers is extremely efficient. Furthermore,

A group of emperor penguins huddles close together to protect themselves against the cold. Most people consider penguins typical animals of the South Pole. All the penguin species are found throughout the Southern Hemisphere. However, only the emperor penguin and the king penguin nest on Antarctica.

A group of Adélie penguins returns to the nesting area by marching across the ice. These penguins feed almost exclusively on krill, which they catch at depths of 230 to 328 feet (70 to 100 m).

the animal spends only a minimum part of its time out of water. The emporer penguin's body is adapted to a life in the ocean. Its considerable insulation represents its greatest limitation.

The penguins of the more temperate areas are smaller than those in the Antarctic. A small body volume per surface area loses more heat than a larger body volume per surface area. The Antarctic penguins have a large body volume per surface area ratio. Thus, they are able to maintain their heat more efficiently than the penguins of the more temperate areas.

During the months in which they are not involved in reproduction on land, the penguins live constantly in the water. They are able to swim with the ease of a dolphin. The penguins legs are kept to the rear of its body and function as a rudder while swimming. The flippers propel the animal through the water.

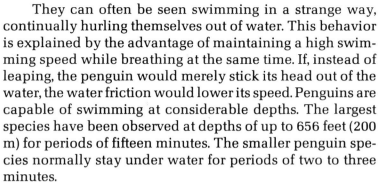

They can often be seen swimming in a strange way, continually hurling themselves out of water. This behavior is explained by the advantage of maintaining a high swimming speed while breathing at the same time. If, instead of leaping, the penguin would merely stick its head out of the water, the water friction would lower its speed. Penguins are capable of swimming at considerable depths. The largest species have been observed at depths of up to 656 feet (200 m) for periods of fifteen minutes. The smaller penguin species normally stay under water for periods of two to three minutes.

(People who regard the adaptations of the penguins as fantastic tend to view the adaptations in the context of the more "normal" temperate climates in which those people live. One would do well to reflect on the relativity of everything to avoid misunderstandings of the natural world.)

The emperor penguin remains motionless for three to four months to incubate its egg under conditions of 90 mile (150 km) per hour winds and a temperature of -76°F (-60°C). However, it is not in danger of freezing. Rather, it would be uncomfortable under more "favorable" conditions. The Antarctic is not a hostile and difficult environment for this animal. Any other location, however, would be.

One should consider all of the advantages of a life in the Antarctic for a bird the penguin's size. Only a few predators attack the penguin or its young. They are the skuas and the jaeger birds, which do not, however, have a significant impact on the populations of the penguin colonies. Furthermore, the penguin has almost unlimited food resources available for the reproductive period. Its populations can reach high levels without damage to the environment.

Few harmful disease germs and parasites are able to complete a full cycle under these environmental conditions. Therefore, the penguin has practically no diseases. Essentially, the Antarctic is the most attractive place on earth for the penguins.

The seven species of antarctic penguins belong to three different genera. The emperor penguin and the king penguin belong to the genus *Aptenodytes*. The Adélie penguin, the chinstrap penguin, and the gentoo penguin belong to the genus *Pygoscelis*. The macaroni penguin and the rockhopper penguin belong to the genus *Eudyptes*.

The gentoo penguin is about 32 inches (80 cm) long and weighs 13 pounds (6 kg). It lives primarily on the islands at the edge of the Antarctic Convergence and has a total

The macaroni penguin nests on most of the islands near the Antarctic continent. The crests of this species are similar to those of the rockhopper penguin.

population of about 350,000. The chinstrap penguin is about 26 inches (67 cm) long and weighs 10 pounds (4.5 kg). In Antarctica, this animal lives almost entirely in the maritime band on the Antarctic Peninsula and the nearby islands. Its total population is somewhere between three and ten million individuals. Its numbers are increasing in the Antarctic, although the species is concentrated in the South American sector.

The Adélie penguin is the best known to visitors of the Antarctic. This is because its populations live on the coasts of the continent within the limit of the pack ice. The Adélie penguin weighs about 11 pounds (5 kg) and is about 28 inches (70 cm) long. Its total population is between five and ten million.

The Adélie, chinstrap, and gentoo penguins nest in large colonies that form every year in the same locations. The reproductive biology is similar for all three species. In October, the majority of the adults of reproductive age are already involved in building the nest. Since few materials are available for this, the birds often steal material from neighboring nests.

Once started, the nest is rarely abandoned. The male and female take turns watching the nest while one or the other feeds in the ocean. In November, mating takes place. Soon afterward, the female then lays two eggs. These eggs must be incubated for from thirty to thirty-five days, and during this period, the male and female take turns entering the ocean to feed. Three to four weeks after hatching, the young are left alone for longer and longer periods. During this time, they gather in groups. These groups offer some protection from the frequent attacks of skua birds. By preying on the weakest young, the skuas have a better chance of succeeding with their hunt, and they minimize their heat loss. The skuas would use up much more energy if they attacked healthy, strong prey. Each parent penguin finds its own young by loud calls. The young penguin is certain to respond to these calls, as it is still dependent on its parents for food. To feed the young, the parents regurgitate the krill that they have eaten. The gentoos, Adélie, and chinstrap penguins feed almost exclusively on the krill they fish at depths of 230 to 328 feet (70 to 100 m).

After about nine weeks of life, the young become fully independent and venture into the water alone. At this time, the parents are now free of their rearing duties. They then undergo the molting of their feathers. This process requires

A normal-colored penguin is pictured with an albino penguin *(foreground)*. All species of penguins occasionally produce rare individuals with yellow or white feathers. This phenomenon is due to changes in the genetic code.

a previous fattening to make up for the lack of adequate feather insulation. Molting lasts for about three or four weeks. At the end of this period, the penguins all return to the water and scatter until the next breeding season.

The Adélie penguins, which live in the more southern regions, must complete all of these phases in less time. The summer is shorter in the areas they inhabit. Their young often leave the colony before they are completely developed physically. Therefore, they have a high death rate. This is especially so for the young that linger too long in the colony. By this time, the weather conditions have become too severe, and the parents can no longer care for them.

The macaroni and rockhopper penguins are easily identified by the colored crests on their heads. The macaroni penguin is 28 inches (70 cm) long and weighs about 9 pounds (4.2 kg). It inhabits all the subantarctic and antarctic islands, but it does not range as far south as the continental coast. It has a total population of perhaps fifteen to twenty million animals. The colonies of macaroni penguins are spectacular. The birds huddle together and seem to be

The rockhopper penguin is a small penguin. It is characterized by two yellow crests on the top of the head.

involved in constant conflicts over territory. The rockhopper penguin is the smallest of the antarctic penguins. It weighs only 5 pounds (2.5 kg) and is 22 inches (55 cm) long. This species lives almost exclusively on the subantarctic islands, where its population numbers in the millions.

Rockhopper and macaroni penguins have similar reproductive habits. These habits partially follow those of the gentoo, Adélie, and chinstrap penguins. In November, the penguins build a nest and lay their eggs. These eggs are incubated from thirty-two to thirty-six days. Both parents cooperate in building the nest and caring for and feeding the young. The macaroni and the rockhopper penguins lay two eggs of different sizes. The first egg is always half the size of the second one. The smaller egg is almost never brooded. When brooding an egg, the adult penguin keeps its eggs warm by covering them with its body. This second egg, because it is not brooded, is discarded. This two-egg feature seems to be the result of a progressive adaptation to the Antarctic environment. This adaptation, however, has not reached its completion, which would be the laying of only one egg. The production and care of one egg, rather than two, saves a considerable amount of energy. It also gives the single chick a greater chance of survival. The rockhopper and macaroni penguins originated in the temperate regions, where the conditions were not as harsh as the Antarctic. Perhaps these penguins were able to spread to and compete in the Antarctic because of this partial "energy-saving" adaptation.

The biology of the emperor and king penguins is much different from that of the above described penguin species. The emperor penguin is a massive bird, with a length of 45 inches (115 cm) and a weight of 66 pounds (30 kg). The king penguin is 37 inches (95 cm) long and weighs only 33 pounds (15 kg). The king penguin lives primarily in the subantarctic band and has a total population of about two million. The emperor penguin lives in continental Antarctica with a total population of not more than thirty thousand individuals. Both species feed on fish and squid and do not eat krill. Each penguin broods its single egg in an upright position, protecting it within a fold of skin between its legs. They do not build nests. Because of their large sizes, they have a varied reproductive cycle.

The king penguins live in colonies throughout the year. In the summer, the colonies are formed primarily by the adults. In the winter, they are made up mostly of the young.

A wandering albatross sits on its nest.
Ten of the thirteen living species of
albatrosses are distributed only in the
Southern Hemisphere.

This illustration shows several marine birds typically found over the Antarctic Ocean. *From left to right, and from top to bottom:* gray-headed albatross, Magellan gull, light-mantled sooty albatross, antarctic petrel, antarctic prion, parasitic jaeger, south polar skua, kelp gull, snow petrel, arctic tern, cape pigeon, antarctic tern, and sheathbill.

These young penguins have immature feathers that are small and light brown in color. Egg laying can occur between November and March. This varies according to when the parents have finished raising the young of the preceding year.

The young bird does not become completely independent before winter sets in. Winter occurs from May to October. This is a critical period for the offspring. Its parents rarely bring food to the young, so it must rely on its fat reserves. In October, the parents resume a more regular feeding of the young, and its development is normally completed by December. Finally, at this point, the female parent can lay another egg. If the egg is laid between January and February, which is the end of summer, the young that hatches will have a poor chance of building up enough fat reserves before winter. The death rate of these late broods is very high. The king penguin, thus, does not have an annual reproductive cycle. In favorable periods, it has two broods every three years. In unfavorable periods, it reproduces once every two years.

The emperor penguin is totally different. This species has an annual cycle, with the young hatching in the warmest season. The egg is laid between May and June. It is held on the legs of the male parent, protected by the fold of the stomach. The male broods the egg for the entire sixty-five days. Adding the courtship period and the time spent searching for the best brooding site, the male remains on land for over two months. This is remarkable, since these events occur during the dead of winter, and the male does not eat during this period. Its weight drops, but not excessively. During courtship the weight loss is 25 percent, and another 15 percent is lost during the brooding period. The weight loss is relatively low because the male sleeps and remains completely inactive during brooding. To conserve body heat, the brooding penguins all huddle together.

As soon as the female returns, the male is free to enter the water and feed. If the young hatches before the female arrives, the male will nourish the young with a substance produced by its stomach. The young penguins grow quickly, and in January or February, its feathers are molted.

THE ANTARCTIC ENVIRONMENT

The estimate of the annual consumption of krill by the various animals and the huge annual production of the krill have been noted. If the annual production of krill is compared to the total annual fish catch, this number becomes even more significant. Previously, great numbers of krill were consumed by the large whale populations. Now that only a few whales are left, it is unclear how much krill can be harvested for human purposes, without causing great imbalances in the environment.

Several factors would indicate that the tremendous availability of krill may be an illusion. The great stability of the Antarctic environment is not immune to the negative effects of excessive tampering from the outside. On the contrary, the Antarctic environment is so fragile that a massive krill harvest would immediately result in a natural imbalance.

The Effects of the Whaling Activities

Because of the great reduction in the number of whales, it would seem that about 150 million tons of krill are now available for other uses. This figure corresponds to the amount of krill previously eaten by the whales. On the other hand, the populations of other animal species have increased in recent decades.

The crab-eating seal, for example, has increased its reproductive capacity. Its population has been growing at an annual rate of 7.5 percent. This has resulted from a lowering of the average age at which the seal reaches sexual maturity. In 1950, this age was four years, but in the early 1970s, it had dropped to a little over two years. When the breeding age drops, the animal populations immediately begin to increase. The Kerguelen fur seal also shows a yearly population increase that is exceptionally high—almost 17 percent. This is once more associated with the greater availability of krill.

The only two whale species that have not been massacred by whalers are the Sei whale and the Minke whale. Both show a distinct lowering of the age of sexual maturity. In the Minke whale, this age dropped from fourteen to six years. This would indicate that the effects of the whaling activities have created a larger space for these other species, which do not have to compete as much for food. Estimating the number of these smaller whales is an extremely difficult task, although there are indications that the population of Minke whales has considerably increased.

Opposite page: Crab-eating seals rest on an ice block in Hope Bay. The increased availability of krill resulting from the reduced populations of whales has brought about an increase in the reproductive rate of the crab-eating seal. Its population increase has now reached 7.5 percent per year.

87

A southern giant petrel tends its nest in the Orkney Islands. This species has a total length of 33 to 36 inches (84 to 92 cm) and a wingspan of over 6 feet (2 m). The southern giant petrel is the largest species of its family, reaching the size of a small albatross. It often follows ships in search of food scraps, and it is always present around carcasses of marine mammals. The southern giant petrel has also been known to attack colonies of penguins, preying on the young and the eggs.

The Adélie, chinstrap, and rockhopper penguins make up the majority of the antarctic birds. Their population is estimated in the tens of millions. Several populations of these species have increased at an annual rate of 6 to 10 percent during the last few decades. The increases are not as notable for the populations found in the Antarctic zones with less krill. This fact, once again, proves the direct relationship between the resource and the consumer.

The population of the king penguin is also increasing, even though this animal feeds on squid, octopuses, and fish. In this case, the relationship with the krill is indirect. Squid, octopuses, and fish are more numerous because of the increase in the krill production. However, it is difficult to estimate the increased numbers of fish because of the influence of the fishing industry on all of the participants involved.

Other animals at the secondary level of krill consumption have increased in number. Examples include the southern giant petrels, which feed on the carcasses of vertebrate animals found on the beaches. The petrels are more numerous because there is a greater availability of abandoned young prey and prey killed accidentally. If one adds up the quantity of krill eaten by these increased animal populations, it appears that the annual renewal of the krill is the same as before.

Annual Consumption of Krill
(in millions of tons)

Year	1900	1984
Whales	190	40
Seals	50	130
Birds	50	130
Fish	100	70
Squid & Octopuses	80	100
Total	470	470

The Commercial Harvest of Krill

According to the estimates, the annual consumption of krill would be about 500 million tons per year. This amount is surprisingly close to the estimated minimum annual production of krill. This finding does not lend support to the new enthusiasm toward harvesting this new sea resource. It leads one to believe that harvesting the krill would be possible provided that it is done cautiously. The catching of krill should be done in limited quantities, which would ensure enough time for the natural elements to adjust to a new balance.

This leaves room for the prospect of a future return of the whale populations to their original levels. The renewal process will not be immediate. It would probably take many years to restore the whales to their original levels, and this may not be possible at all.

THE SUBANTARCTIC ISLANDS

In the Atlantic and Indian ocean sectors, the continent of Antarctica is surrounded by a ring of small islands located between 46 and 59 degrees south latitude. The islands are either solitary, such as Macquarie and Bouvetoya, or they belong to small island groups, such as the Kerguelen Islands and the South Sandwich Islands. These islands are not covered by the legal restrictions of the Antarctic Treaty of 1959, which was initially signed by twelve nations with four more joining later.

The subantarctic islands are under the sovereignty of several different nations. These include Norway, Great Britain, France, Australia, and South Africa.

As mentioned before, the islands have different origins. Several, such as South Georgia, were originally part of a continent. Others, such as the Kerguelen Islands, were formed by volcanic activity. The Kerguelen Islands are at least 100 million years old. Macquarie is only 5 million years old. The islands of Marion and Prince have lava rock formations that are 276,000 years old. Probably, all these islands were once found within the Antarctic Convergence, which in the past was located farther north. The landscape of the islands shows evidence of the action of ancient glaciers, which no longer exist on the islands.

Plants and Animals

The climate and, consequently, the plants and animals of the subantarctic islands are influenced by their position in respect to the Convergence. Bouvetoya and the South Sandwich Islands are almost completely covered by ice. Only 15 percent of Heard is ice free. South Georgia is 40 percent ice free, and the Kerguelens are 80 percent. The other islands are almost completely free of ice. The lack of ice is made up for by the high amount of rainfall the islands receive. They are covered by clouds almost all of the year and are continuously subjected to strong winds from the west.

The biology of these islands is interesting for two reasons. The study of the plant and animal species on the islands enables one to reconstruct the relationships and similarities among the neighboring islands. This results in a greater understanding of the geological evolution of the Southern Hemisphere. The second reason is that, unlike the continent of Antarctica, the islands have been inhabited by people for a longer time. They were especially frequented in the whaling and seal hunting days, when they were used as

Opposite page: Reindeer wander the pastures at Hlisvik on the island of South Georgia. The introduction of foreign plant-eating mammals into the local environments has greatly damaged the fragile vegetation of the subantarctic islands. In several cases, these introductions have led to the extinction of native species and subspecies of animals that are not able to compete with the new animals.

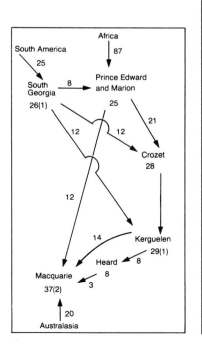

Illustrated are biogeographic relationships of the flowering plants on the subantarctic islands. The number of species is indicated for each island, and the figures within parentheses refer to the number of native species. The numbers with arrows indicate the number of species that are common between two different islands or nearby continents.

bases by the hunters. This human presence, however, has caused considerable imbalances in the natural environments of the islands.

The islands have a larger variety of plants than the continent, although shrubs and trees do not grow there. Generally, the islands have many more species of seed-bearing plants than the continent, including twenty-four species of grasses. Of course, there are hundreds of species of mosses, liverworts, and lichens.

For the most part, the island plants show similarities with those of the South American continent. Fossils of the southern beech tree have been found on several islands. This tree is typical of Tasmania and also Tierra del Fuego, an island group separated from the southern tip of Argentina by the Strait of Magellan. This fossil evidence suggests that these lands were once all joined in the supercontinent of Gondwana. From South Georgia, which is the island closest to Tierra del Fuego, all the way to the other end of the subantarctic island ring, one finds fewer and fewer species. These species are typical of Tierra del Fuego, and the islands have at least some species common to that region. Macquarie Island, being closest to Australia and farthest from South America, has a predominance of species that originated in Australia. Many species are native, but a fair percentage is also widely distributed in other lands. Other species have been transported there by humans during the successive colonizations of the islands. For example, the spear grass *Poa cookii* is native to the subantarctic region. Another species of spear grass, *Poa annua*, has been introduced into South Georgia Island. Today, this type of spear grass is one of the most widespread species on the island.

The animals of the subantarctic islands have an even more complicated history of interventions and controls. The original land animals of the islands were exclusively invertebrates. Without counting the protozoans, rotifers, and tardigrades, 387 species of invertebrates have been described. These include 22 species of nematode worms, 3 mollusks, 4 flatworms, 210 insects, 144 spiders, 1 crustacean, and 2 myriapods, which are centipedelike animals. However, the invertebrates are a long way from being completely studied. Several islands are rarely visited and are practically unknown. Much research remains to be done, especially if one considers all the interesting rock formations that resulted from the movement of the earth's crust.

King penguins gather on South Georgia Island.

Following pages: A pair of great skuas in the Orkneys signals their territory by displaying their intimidating behavior.

Many studies have been done on animal groups that are highly resistant to the extreme antarctic conditions. These studies, done on such animals as springtails, mites, and ticks, reveal a distribution pattern that is similar to that of plants. It also reveals the presence of many animal species that can be compared to the animals of ancient Gondwana. The mites are ideal study animals for analyzing the relationships between different lands. (The mites were discussed earlier in relation to their colonization of the antarctic nunataks.)

The variety of the animal communities is closely related to average low temperatures. The temperatures influence the vegetation, which in turn influences the number of animals that each island can support. Some of the vertebrate animals that inhabit the islands have already been mentioned. These include Kerguelen fur seals, elephant seals, several species of penguins, and the marine

93

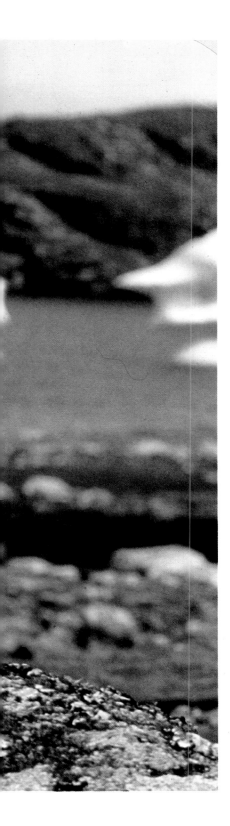

birds that nest there. Only four species of small land birds are native to the islands.

Animals Introduced by Humans

The most conspicuous animals of the subantarctic islands are those that have been introduced by people. Introduction is done both accidentally and deliberately. At least fifteen different species have been brought to these lands, and only some have succeeded in adapting. Many species of domestic animals were not able to survive despite the repeated attempts of whalers to introduce them. Attempts were made to introduce cattle, horses, donkeys, mules, goats, pigs, and dogs. With time, however, all of them have completely disappeared. Among the accidental introductions are the house mice, Norway rats, and the black rats.

The Effects of Animal Introductions

The introduction of such foreign species into these fragile and poor environments had an inevitable disturbing effect on the preexisting natural balance. The damages that resulted from these introductions were enormous. The new herbivores practically eliminated all the most appetizing plants. The resultant lack of plant cover then led to faster erosion of the soil. The reduction of the vegetation also had the negative effect of reducing the number of suitable nesting sites for marine birds. Furthermore, the nesting marine birds were hunted by the new predators.

During the periods when the marine birds were not nesting, the predators survived by preying on the new herbivores of the islands. This situation created a complex web of interrelated effects. The numerous rabbits on Macquarie, for example, destroyed a large part of the most delicate vegetation. As the number of rabbits grew, so did the populations of their predators, such as cats and skuas. Both the cats and the skuas are also responsible for the great reduction in the numbers of bird colonies.

The upsetting of ancient balances even caused the elimination of some native species. The most conspicuous losses have been two native bird species of Macquarie: the crested parakeet and a subspecies of the New Zealand rail. Both species managed to survive for seventy years after the introduction of the cat, but they became extinct after the introduction of the rabbit.

So far, the attempts to rid the islands of the unwanted "guests" have all been unsuccessful.

PATAGONIA AND TIERRA DEL FUEGO

In the concluding pages of The *Voyage of the Beagle*, Charles Darwin attempted to explain why Patagonia had impressed him so much more than any other natural wonder he had seen. Darwin was hauntingly reminded of the virgin forests of Tierra del Fuego and Southern Chile, "where death and decay prevail." He also recalled the plains of the Argentinean Patagonia: "Regarded by everyone as desolate and useless, and described in negative terms—without dwellings, without water, without trees, without mountains. Why, then, do these arid desert expanses haunt my memory? I think it is because here the flight of fantasy is entirely free." Still in 1830, at the time of the historic voyage of the *Beagle* (the ship on which Darwin sailed), these lands were "almost unreachable and therefore unknown. As they appear today, they show signs of having endured for interminable epochs, and it does not appear that there is a limit to their future duration."

Darwin's words set the stage for a description of this frontier land, an account of the explorers, and a discussion of the complex mosaic of the vegetation and animals that characterize this region. Its location is interesting, situated between the forest of the Andes Mountains, the blue ice of the Antarctic, and the almost treeless grassland area of Argentina (the pampas).

A Land of Monsters

Patagonia is at the extreme southern edge of South America. It is a triangle that widens in a northward direction, between 40° and 55° south latitude. For centuries, this region was represented on maps as the last land. This was, of course, before the continent of Antarctica was discovered. On medieval maps, Patagonia was labeled simply with the word "Fog." Students of the ancient Greek philosopher and mathematician Pythagoras referred to Patagonia as an upside-down world where the snow moved upwards and the sun shone with black light. Up until 1619, when the Dutch fleet of Shouten and Le Maire rounded Cape Horn, the mapmakers drew Tierra del Fuego as the northern tip of Antarctica. They drew mermaids and monsters all around it. These monsters included ugly women with snakes for hair as well as rocs, which were legendary birds of prey having enormous size and strength. The ancient maps of South America always showed an arm of the sea separating the South American continent from the land of fog and monsters. It is remarkable that this body of

Opposite page: Lakes and glaciers are typical features of the Patagonian landscape. The large glacier Perito Francisco P. Moreno ends in the water of Lake Argentino. By navigating along the Brazo Rico and the Canal de los Tempanos, one can observe the effects of the glacier's movements. In periods when the ice advances, the water of the Brazo Rico rises. This is due to a movement of ice that blocks the narrow arm of the lake. Consequently, vast areas of southern beech forests are destroyed by flooding. In this area, snow is plentiful even in the summer. The icebergs and the winding arms of the lakes give one the feeling of being among the fiords of Norway.

Patagonia begins as far north as Rio Colorado. This area is characterized by sedimentary rock formations. From the Rio Colorado to the Rio Negro, across the grassland called the pampas, the sedimentary rocks are progressively substituted by layers of pebbles. The mesetas are gigantic areas of tableland sloping toward the Atlantic Ocean. They are composed of sedimentary rock deposits alternating with layers of solidified lava. The western sector of Patagonia is composed of the Andes mountain chain plus a system of islands, which begins to the north at Chiloé. This island system extends south all the way to Cape Horn. Actually, this island series can be considered a mountain chain that is partially submerged in the ocean.

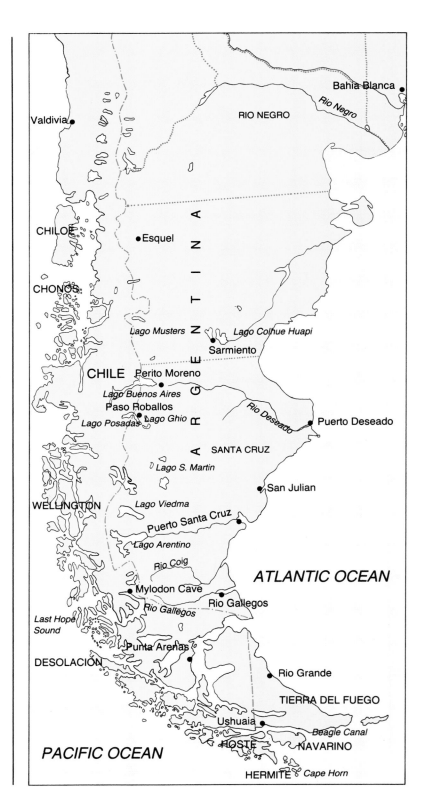

This map shows Patagonia's vegetation zones. Between Rio Colorado and Rio Negro, the vegetation consists of a treeless grassland *(indicated by wavy lines)*. This vegetation is related to the wooded plains of Northern Argentina *(indicated by vertical lines)*. The typical vegetation of the Argentinean Patagonia consists of a dry and discontinuous grassland *(indicated by area with small circles)*. Few low shrubs and spiny low bushes grow in this region. The Argentinean side has been separated from the Chilean side since ancient times, due to the raising of the Andes Mountains. The climatic differences between the two sides explain the great variety of vegetation of the southern Andes *(indicated by area with diagonal lines)*. Of the 150 species of cacti that are found in Argentina, only four or five are present in Chile. On the Pacific coast, south of the coastal deserts of Chile (34° south latitude), one finds a semiarid wooded land. There are also some relatively dry forest areas *(indicated by horizontal lines)*. The only conifer tree found in this zone is the *Araucaria araucan* pine. The thicker and more humid forests begin around 40° south latitude. The forest of the Valdivia Province *(dotted area)* has various species of beeches and larches and a rich undergrowth of liana vines, epiphytes, ferns, mosses, and bamboo. Farther south, one finds the Chilean beech forest and the Magellanic forest *(area indicated by uniform gray)*, with deciduous tree species and heath shrubs.

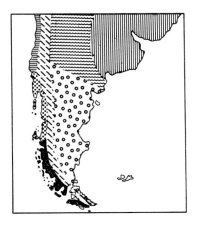

water, later known as the "Strait of Magellan," was represented on the maps before it was actually discovered.

The boring narration of Antonio Pigafetta, the chronicler on board Magellan's ship, suddenly becomes colorful in the pages describing the approach to Patagonia in 1520. As the ship neared land at San Julian (between Rio Deseado and Rio Chico), the crew saw a giant dancing naked on the shore. The giant was "dancing and leaping and, while singing, throwing sand and dust on his head." As the Europeans came before him, he covered himself with a guanaco hide. This "giant" was one of the Tehuelche Indians. These copper-skinned natives were called "men of the South." Pigafetta wrote that they ran faster than horses and hunted with bows and arrows, using sharpened stones for arrowheads. He also wrote that "they roared like bulls" and lived a nomadic life "like gypsies." Supposedly, Magellan made the exclamation "Ha, patagonia," which means "big foot," upon seeing the natives' large moccasins. And thus, supposedly, was born the name *Patagonia*.

Patagonia, or "land of the giants," extends for more than 347,400 sq. miles (900,000 sq. km) into parts of Argentina and Chile. This region includes several types of environments. There are vast grass-covered plateaus, called the "pampas," on the arid Atlantic side, east of the Andes mountain range. There is a strip of forests, lakes, and glaciers along the humid Pacific coast and the Andes mountain chain. Finally, there is the large island of Tierra del Fuego. The western part of this island is the continuation of the Andes, with peaks rising over 5,905 feet (1,800 m) above sea level. The eastern zone of Tierra del Fuego is characterized by the same flatness found on the Atlantic side of Patagonia.

The Strait of Magellan can be considered a mountain pass at sea level. The fiords and canals of the jagged western coast represent the valleys of the Andes mountain chain. The steep islands are actually the tops of immersed peaks of the mountain chain.

The Desert

After crossing the Rio Colorado on the pampas, one notices sedimentary rock formations (formed from deposits of river sediments) followed by layers of round pebbles and soft sandstones. These layers are predominant in the Rio Negro valley, where the river makes a wide cut across the vast tableland. "If we consider that all of these pebbles, as countless as the grains of sand in a desert, are derived from

In the Province of Chubut along the road that runs from Esquel to Sarmiento, one finds Patagonia's vast grassland. This zone is arid and windy, with a scattered grass cover, low shrubs, clumps of compact bushes, and cacti. The western part of the Patagonian grassland is not as dry, and it is characterized by a plant community with different species.

the slow process of rocks falling on the ancient coasts and riverbeds," wrote Charles Darwin, "if we consider that these fragments have been crumbled to pieces, slowly rounded and rolled, and transported long distances, the mind is boggled when thinking of the extremely long passage of time that was necessary for this work." It is mind boggling and fascinating.

To the south, the grassland becomes more and more barren and arid. The sandy soil, mixed with gravel and lacking organic matter, lacks a continuous cover of vegetation. There are clumps of dry brown spear grass and bent grass, as well as scattered low bushes with spines. The brush

looks like a grayish green sea, with clouds of white dust that the wind raises up from the "salinas." The salinas are seasonal lakes in the area of Bahia Blanca, the last city before the desert begins.

In the summer, the salinas are transformed into fields of white salt. Some parts of the land look as though they are covered with snow. The whiteness of the salt fields is sharply contrasted by the dark and desolate plains, which occasionally are colored by pink flocks of flamingos.

The Rio Negro is the biogeographic boundary of Patagonia. Neither the viscachia rodent of the pampas, nor the common rhea bird, which is a ground bird of the northern plains similar to an ostrich, has spread south beyond this "border." At the mouth, the gleaming river flows between cliffs that are as white as bone, with emerald strips of cultivated land on each side. Farther south, the Rio Chubut crosses a checkerboard of irrigated fields. These fields, which have replaced the original desert areas, are protected from the wind by rows of poplar trees.

This region looks like a miniature Nile River valley. Vast expanses of "mesetas" surround the green strips of vegetation that border the rivers. Mesetas are terraced plateaus that rise in steps from the Atlantic Ocean. These sedimentary tablelands were formed by deposits between 63 and 230 million years ago. Here and there, volcano cones dot the landscape. The lava sheets that flowed from these volcanoes solidified into layers of basaltic rock. In 1832, Darwin described the Patagonian mesetas: "Pleasant dry weather and the splendid blue sky is rarely hidden by clouds. Standing in the middle of one of these desert plains and looking toward the interior, one usually sees a slope that supports another plain that is higher and just as smooth and desolate. On all of the other sides, the horizon is blurred by the flickering mirage that rises from the burning surface."

After a century and a half, the landscape is still much the same. Perhaps the only change is the addition of fences that have been built for the extensive raising of sheep. This activity was begun in 1890 by the predominately British colonists.

The air in Patagonia is dry because the rain clouds that form over the Pacific Ocean are not able to cross the mountain chain. Thus, proceeding east from the forest of the Andes Mountains slopes, one encounters an infertile grassland that becomes a near-desert near the Atlantic coast. This is the combined result of the Andes Mountains and the

Illustrated is a group of multicolored South American ducks. Almost all of them are native to the pampas and Patagonia. Except for one species that is exclusively marine, they have unique adaptations to a life in the grasslands. Although they are extensively hunted, these ducks are still widespread and common. This may be the result of the increased grassland areas used by sheep ranchers. It may also be related to the decline of the fox population. The foxes normally prey on young ducks and eggs of these birds. These ducks are *(from left to right, and from top to bottom)* the gray-headed duck, native to western Patagonia where it nests on coastal islands running from Chile to Cape Horn; the red-headed duck, native to Tierra del Fuego and the Falkland Islands; the Magellan duck, with a strong difference in the coloration of the male and female; and the kelp duck, which feeds on ocean algae during low tides.

cold ocean current of the Falkland Islands, which arrives from the south. These factors create a subdesert climate that is similar to that of the Peruvian coasts and the Chilean highlands. The area is subject to considerable freezing, as the temperature can drop to a low of -4 F (-20 C). The annual precipitation, which is about 8 inches (20 cm) over the Rio Negro, is as low as 4 inches (9.4 cm) over the Rio Chubut and Santa Cruz. The typical plants of the dry areas are cacti and various other plants that can tolerate dry conditions.

Along the rivers and in the areas that receive the humid western winds, one finds green patches of pepper trees and strips of forest. The vegetation interrupts the sterile yellow color of the Patagonian grassland. South of Rio Gallegos, the grasslands are greener and more fertile. The farmhouses of British settlers are more numerous in this area. They are usually painted in bright colors and surrounded by greenhouses and flower beds.

The Inhabitants of the Desert

One should not think of the Patagonian desert as an infinite expanse of sand dunes. To use the words of Bruce

The guanacos were common on the plains and plateaus of Argentina until 1880, the era of European colonization. Due to the increased cultivation, the fencing off of pastureland, and hunting, their numbers have diminished. Today, they can be seen in the most remote areas of Patagonia and in the environments at the foot of the Andes Mountains. The photograph shows a group of guanacos in the grassland of southern Patagonia. This is probably a small family group, consisting of a male accompanied by a few females and their young.

Chatwin, writer and scholar of nomadic populations, it is "a low thicket of gray-leaved thorns which give off a bitter smell when crushed. There was no sound but the wind, whirring through thorns and whistling through dead grass, and no other sign of life but a hawk, and a black beetle easing over white stones."

The animal population is as meager as the plant community. The numerous rodents of the grassland are hidden. Their presence is barely hinted at by the maze of tunnels that are dug by the tucu-tuco rodents and the southern guinea pigs. The tucu-tucos derived their name from the alarm cries they make in case of danger. These cries echo through the tunnels.

Occasionally, one may happen upon an agouti, a solitary rodent that is active during the day. When disturbed, the agouti bristles its thick reddish brown fur, which has the effect of making it appear larger. Sometimes, one may encounter a group of mara rodents, which are similar to guinea pigs. However, they look more like hares when they flee with irregular hops across the grasses.

In the sky, one can spot vulture hawks as they slowly glide in circles. Their flight is suddenly interrupted when they quickly dive and pounce on such prey as small hawks.

Lake Argentino, from which Rio Santa Cruz originates, and Lake Buenos Aires are the largest lakes of the Andes Mountains in Patagonia. The lengths of many Andean lakes are situated in an east-west direction. The lakes are found along the course of deep valleys created by the past glaciers. Many of the lakes are long and slender. The photograph was taken from the north slopes of the arid peak of Campo Anita, which is covered by a grassland and dense, low-growing bushes. The low growth of the bushes is an adaptation to the wind.

This is the case whether the prey is alive or already dead. Occasionally yellow-tufted ibises can be seen moving among the pasturing animals. These large, long-legged birds are characterized by a bright pink color and a melancholy call.

Darwin further wrote that "the curse of sterility hangs over this land, and not even the water that runs in its bed of pebbles can escape it. There are few aquatic birds because almost no food is available in these sterile rivers."

Nevertheless, several aquatic birds have adapted to the

grassland environments, adopting a diet mainly composed of grasses. There are several species of multicolored ducks that are native to Patagonia. They strongly resemble geese due to their short, narrow beaks. The gray-headed duck has a brown and black plumage decorated with ornate designs. The red-headed duck is smaller in size. The male Magellan duck is white with black stripes on the back and sides. The female is reddish brown with black stripes and is less showy than the male. Although they are able swimmers, these birds spend most of their time on land. They feed on grasses, and the females lay their eggs in clumps of grass. Local sheep ranchers claim that six wild ducks eat as much grass as one sheep. As a result, the ducks are extensively hunted.

The Patagonian seed snipe is exclusively vegetarian and nests on the ground. This bird has an irregular flight and a mournful call. The seed snipes's eggs are dust colored, and each time the female moves away from the eggs, she first covers them with soil. Immediately after the eggs hatch, the female removes all traces of egg shell from the nest area and attempts to cover the active chicks with blades of grass. This behavior is used to keep predators from being attracted to the nesting area.

The guanaco is probably the most conspicuous presence on the grassland. This animal belongs to the camel family and is similar to the llama. The guanacos spread to Patagonia from Southern Bolivia. Occasionally, one can observe them standing on top of a hill, pasturing in groups, or fleeing in file along the sides of a meseta. They have elegant profiles, with long necks and extended ears. Groups of young, nomadic males sometimes number over fifty animals. A typical family normally includes five to ten individuals and is composed of an adult male, several females, and the young.

Guanacos are social and territorial animals, marking the boundaries of their territory with piles of manure. In the past, the Indians used this manure for fuel. It seems that the guanacos choose the areas where they want to die. Darwin described unique cemeteries along the banks of the Rio Santa Cruz and the Rio Gallegos. Here, the soil is white with skeletons. However, the skeletons could also have been left from the hunting of these animals by nomadic Indian tribes, the Puelche of the north and the Tehuelche of the south. The guanaco was as important to these Indians as the buffalo was to the Indians of the North American plains.

An old male guanaco or other member of the group

Ancient animals called the megatherium, the mylodon, and the glyptodont were toothless animals. They commonly inhabited South America up to ten thousand years ago. The living animals that are related to them are the three-toed sloths (related to the giant ground sloth megatherium and the mylodon) and the armadillos (related to the glyptodont). The interruption of the Isthmus of Panama about fifty million years ago resulted in the separation of South American animals from the North American ones. Through millions of years, the animals kept evolving. When the two continents were later reunited (between three and five million years ago), many South American animal groups had evolved species that were often gigantic. These giant species were not able to compete when the North American animals arrived from the north. Therefore, they became extinct. Several giant species were able to survive to the last ice age. They were commonly hunted by the Patagonian Indians. *From left to right:* an artist's recreation of the giant ground sloth megatherium; the outer shell and skeleton of a glyptodont, which lived in South America in the Pleistocene period (11,000-500,000 years ago); and the skeleton of a mylodon, which was a large sloth that was smaller than the giant ground sloth.

take turns as guard. In the event of danger, they make loud alarm calls, similar to the voice of a crying baby. The group immediately flees, following habitual trails at a light gallop. They move so fast that a person on horseback cannot keep up with them.

Occasionally, among the groups of guanacos, one can see long-billed rheas. These brown birds are smaller than the common rheas and inhabit the areas south of the Rio Negro river. Since rheas flee at the slightest sign of danger, they act as a further "sentry" for the guanacos. A similar situation occurs in Africa where ostriches can be found in mixed groups with zebras and gazelles.

Yet, when a solitary guanaco sees a person on foot, it may stop and stare and gradually approach the person. This occurred to Bruce Chatwin while walking along the dusty road of Lake Blanco. He wrote in his notebook: "You saw him a hundred yards off, a single male, bigger and more graceful than a llama, with his orange coat and white upstanding tail. Guanacos are shy animals, you were told, but this one was mad for you. And when you could walk no more and laid out your sleeping bag, he was there gurgling and sniveling and keeping the same distance. In the morning he was right up close, but the shock of you getting out of your skin was too much for him. That was the end of a friendship, and you watched him bouncing away over a thorn bush like a galleon in a following sea."

Lakes, Glaciers, and Extinct Giants

Westward toward the interior from the Atlantic coast, a series of large lakes interrupts the gray grasslands that cover the eastern side of the Andes. This area is cold and arid, with a considerable difference between the daily high and low temperatures. The Andes Mountains stand out clearly over

The mixed beech forest, which covers a large portion of the small island Redonda in the Beagle Channel, offers an interesting example of parasitism. The branches of the southern beech tree are covered by clumps of a mistletoelike plant. This plant feeds on the nutrients produced by the tree. Around the small Lake Escondido, the forest and the undergrowth are very rich. The cinnamon tree as well as the Magellan gooseberry are common in these mountain environments. On the north side of the island where the humidity is low, one finds the antarctic beech tree. The forest becomes thinner farther up toward the peak of Redonda Island, which has an elevation of 656 feet (200 m). Near the top, vegetation consists of bushes and low shrubs. At the top is a discontinuous grass cover over bare rock. This small island is a good example of the variety of plant communities of the Tierra del Fuego island group. The different environments result from different exposures, the influence of the winds and ocean, the presence of lakes, and the complex landscapes.

the plateaus like a distant blue-and-white curtain. There are forty lakes that cover an area of over 20 sq. miles (50 sq. km). They are located along the border of Chile and Argentina and are included within the large protected areas of Lanin, Nahuel Huapi, Lake Puelo, Los Alerces, and Los Glaciares. These areas are the habitat of the Andean condor, the puma, and the Andean deer. The Andean deer is rare even in the reserves.

Andean lakes are longer when they flow in an east-west direction, following the course of the deep valleys that

A colony of about 1.5 million nesting penguins lives at Punta Tombo in the province of Chubut. The penguins mate for life. Each pair occupies and defends a very small piece of land where the 3-foot (1 m) deep nest is dug. Normally, two eggs are laid around October. They are incubated primarily by the female and hatch between November and December. In the period soon after, a group of newborns is guarded by an adult while the other adults gather a large amount of fish to feed the offspring. (At these latitudes, the young require a large amount of food energy.) This is an example of developed social behavior. The colony scatters in April with the arrival of the winter cold. The penguins winter in the South Atlantic Ocean, off the coasts of Brazil, and return to the Patagonian coasts in the summer. An adult can weigh almost 11 pounds (5 kg) and reach a length of 20 inches (50 cm).

have been dug by glaciers. The lakes are surrounded by glaciers that are thousands of years old, as well as by accumulations of boulders and stones the glaciers transported and deposited.

Despite the fact that the glaciers have retreated considerably, they still occupy an area of over 1,930 sq. miles (5,000 sq. km) in Patagonia. On the Chilean side, tongues of blue ice reach the ocean. Here, summers are cold and cloudy, and the precipitation is abundant. These factors, along with a low rate of evaporation, result in a low snow line in the mountains.

It is not surprising that in past centuries various expeditions journeyed to this region of glacial lakes, searching around Paso Roballos for the legendary city of gold. This is where several voyagers described seeing a fortress of silver and gold at the foot of a volcano, which overlooked a beautiful lake. The atmosphere of the lake area fully justifies this legend. The impressive plateau of the vast Lake Buenos Aires, which is over 772 sq. miles (2,000 sq. km), rises up from Paso Roballos. The plateau was formed by successive layers of pink and green lava flows, appearing almost like an enormous flag when seen from the lowland.

A milky river flows into Lake Ghio, whose shores are of a blinding white color. In the shoals of the opal blue water, there are pink flamingos and thousands of black-necked swans.

When seen from the altitude of Cerro de los Indios, the Posadas and Purreydon lakes form a turquoise strip between the purple rocks. The Cerro de los Indios is a block of red and green volcanic rock where every rock ledge is covered by Indian paintings of hunting scenes. They were painted ten thousand years ago with the use of red earth pigments known as "ocher." "The Indians had chosen the place with an unfaltering eye for the sacred," writes Chatwin on the Indian paintings. "The sky was a hard thin blue and the two circling black dots were condors. Alone on its rockface, [the] unicorn had a thick neck and tapering body. Underneath was a votive shrine with offerings—a tin of Nest's milk, a plaster model of a girl in bed, a nail dipped in gray paint, and some burned-out candles."

The Patagonian unicorn may merely be a legend or a religious belief. However, there is evidence showing that several thousand years ago the Indians still hunted the mylodon. This was a huge ground sloth that ate only plants and inhabited the prairies of South America. The mylodon

A group of South American sea lions swims in the Strait of Magellan near the coast of Santa Maria Island. The presence of various species of carnivorous seals reflects the great numbers of fish in these waters. Elephant seals, southern fur seals, and South American sea lions live in colonies along the coasts of Patagonia. The southern fur seals have been widely hunted in the past. The South American sea lion is the most numerous species. The large males of this species are the first to land on the coasts during the breeding season. They occupy territories within which one male dominates and defends a group of females. Fighting between males is many times restricted to menacing behavior. However, these confrontations may lead to violent fights. South American sea lions feed exclusively on fish, eating 55 to 110 pounds (25 to 50 kg) per day. When the young are big enough to swim, the colony scatters, leaving the beaches deserted until the next breeding season.

became extinct about fifteen thousand years ago. Throughout the 1800s, there were successive findings of bones and remains of mylodons in the ravines of Patagonia. Several fossil experts, or paleontologists, found what they believed was a sort of stall used to keep mylodons as a food stock for the winter. This stall was found in the cavern of Last Hope Sound in the Chilean part of Patagonia.

Another giant ground sloth that is now extinct was the *Megatherium*. This animal was described by naturalist Baron Cuvier as something that was imperfectly created by nature as a joke. It was 16 feet (5 m) long, with large jaws and strong paws armed with claws.

The glyptodon was an enormous armadillo with a tail covered with spikes. The body was enclosed in a bony shell that seems to have been used as a roof by the Tehuelche Indians. The Indian names of several locations in Patagonia prove that these huge animals lived until relatively recent times.

When traveling through these regions, one cannot help but be impressed by the signs of the past. The environment here has not been altered and retains signs of an ancient history. The petrified forest in the province of Santa Cruz probably dates back 140 million years. This was before the Andes Mountains rose and when the humidity was much greater, even on the Atlantic side of Patagonia. There are still some standing trunks of the native pine, which are over 328 feet (100 m) tall and 11 feet (3.5 m) in diameter. These standing trunks, as well as the fallen ones, were petrified by a covering of volcanic ash. They are isolated reminders of the ancient forests among the treeless landscape of the Patagonian grasslands.

Forests Along the Ocean

To find the large forests, apart from the green zones along the sides of several mountains, it is necessary to cross the crest of the Andes mountain chain. The western side has rain forests with average annual precipitation that reaches a record 29 feet (9,000 mm) in some places. The forest in the province of Valdivia is "a scene of death and desolation," to use Darwin's description. It is an intricate world of liana vines, ferns, mosses, bamboo, and epiphytes (plants that grow on other plants, not for food but for support). There are thick layers of decaying tree trunks among the large trees. Two species of southern beech trees grow in this region, as well as the cinnamon tree and the Patagonian larch tree, which reaches a height of 197 feet (60 m). John Byron, a British admiral and grandfather of the famous poet, thus described the rainy coasts of Chile: "Any penetration into the forests is not only extremely difficult, but also dangerous. This is not so much because of the wild beasts, since the area is even difficult for them, but rather because of the deep marshes that make up a large part of this country. The trees seem to be floating rather than growing."

In southern areas, the Chilean beech is the dominant tree. It is also found on the extremely distant coast of New Zealand. This coincidence is further evidence of the theory supporting the existence of the supercontinent Gondwana.

On the mountain slopes that are most exposed to the strong western winds, the beech forest is found in the sheltered areas of ravines and recesses. The Patagonian grassland covers the area between the mountains of Paine and Punta Arenas. This area is sheltered from the direct climatic influence of the ocean by a network of fiords and canals.

The Escollo Eclaireus de los Cormoranos, facing the Beagle Channel, is a well-known nesting location for cormorants. The most common bird here is the blue-eyed cormorant, which forms incredibly dense colonies. The nests are built with dried grass that is soaked in the ocean water. This grass is pasted to the ground with the bird's dung. Both the male and female share in the incubation of the eggs, as well as the feeding and rearing of the young. Four other species of cormorants are found in Patagonia. Each species occupies a different habitat within the environment.

Tierra del Fuego

Along the Strait of Magellan from east to west, the coast is at first flat and gray. The desert grassland of Argentina reaches all the way to the ocean and partially covers the largest island of Patagonia, Tierra del Fuego. Beyond the orange-and-white striped lighthouse of the First Strait and Cape Negro of the Second Strait, the horizon becomes darker. The landscape suddenly changes, taking on "the dark and melancholy aspect of the Chilean coast," to use the

words of Darwin. "Black trees, whitened by snow, can barely be seen through the very fine rain." On rare days the fog lifts, and the strait becomes a flat expanse of blue. On these occasions one can see glaciers and mountains. Mount Sarmiento, which is over 7,546 feet (2,300 m) in elevation, actually appears to be lower, because the entire mountain mass can be seen at one glance from the water to the top of the peak. The name *Tierra del Fuego* derives from the camp fires that the Indians used to make.

GUIDE TO AREAS OF NATURAL INTEREST

One might say that Antarctica is one large park, in the sense that all human activities are strictly controlled there. However, it is not a park in the familiar sense of the word, for the few areas that are particularly protected are not in the same category as the supervised parks in the rest of the world. In Antarctica, there is no recognized sovereignty, and each country refuses to permit inequalities in the management of different areas of territory.

In recent years, a small number of tourists has begun to visit the Antarctic, although not on a regular basis. Aside from the organized flights leaving from New Zealand and the few "private" visitors to the scientific bases, the only regular tourist activity up to now consisted of the cruises of two ocean liners. These ships navigate in the waters off the Antarctic Peninsula and allow brief land visits. But since it is known how fragile the rare land environments of the Antarctic are, even this minor tourist activity has been cause for worry. For one thing, the land visits always take place in the same locations, and these locations are often near colonies of nesting marine birds. The birds, however, are not the main reason for the zones selected. Landing spots are not chosen so much for their naturalistic importance but rather for their accessibility.

The situation is slightly different for the subantarctic islands. In fact, they are managed by particular administrations that are under the jurisdiction of a ruling nation. For example, Macquarie Island is a national park of the Australian federal government. Other islands are completely uninhabited and can be visited by whoever manages to reach them.

Generally, these islands are frequented only by military ships and planes or by workers involved with scientific bases and research. The independent visitor is not able to use these means of transportation to reach the islands. South Georgia is more regularly visited since it is near the Falkland Islands, from which commercial airplanes depart. But access to visitors is strictly regulated. In theory, it is not forbidden to land on such islands as McDonald or Heard. But in practice, in order to reach the majority of the subantarctic islands, it is necessary to have an ocean-going polar ship or a specialized airplane.

The parks and reserves of the extreme southern part of the South American continent are more accessible, though nevertheless still remote. These are located in Argentina, Chile, and the Falkland Islands.

Opposite page: The tourist ship *Linblad Explorer*, which offers cruises of the antarctic islands, was photographed from a ship that supplies the antarctic bases. In the background are the slopes of the crater of Deception Island in the Shetland Island group. The volcano of Deception rose up from the ocean floor. The crater is abotour the Antarctic. Hidden volcanic activity melts the snow in certain patches rather early in the spring. This enables the kelp duck to nest here a month earlier than in the Falkland Islands.

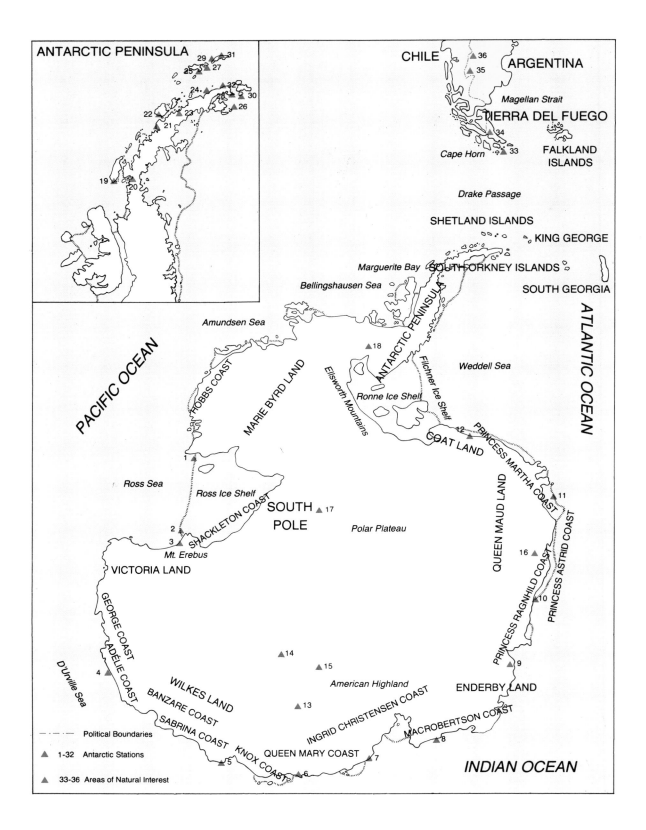

ANTARCTIC PENINSULA

29 ▲31
27
25 ▲
24 ▲32
23 30
22 26
21

19 ▲20

CHILE ▲36 ARGENTINA
35

Magellan Strait

TIERRA DEL FUEGO

▲34 FALKLAND
Cape Horn ▲33 ISLANDS

Drake Passage

SHETLAND ISLANDS

KING GEORGE

Marguerite Bay SOUTH ORKNEY ISLANDS

Bellingshausen Sea SOUTH GEORGIA

Amundsen Sea

ATLANTIC OCEAN

ANTARCTIC PENINSULA

▲18

Weddell Sea

Filchner Ice Shelf

PACIFIC OCEAN

HOBBS COAST

MARIE BYRD LAND

Ellsworth Mountains

Ronne Ice Shelf

COAT LAND

PRINCESS MARTHA COAST

▲12

1 ▲

QUEEN MAUD LAND

11

Ross Sea

Ross Ice Shelf

SHACKLETON COAST

SOUTH POLE ▲17

Polar Plateau

PRINCESS ASTRID COAST

2 ▲
3 ▲

Mt. Erebus

16 ▲

PRINCESS RAGNHILD COAST

VICTORIA LAND

10 ▲

GEORGE COAST

ADÉLIE COAST

▲14

▲15

American Highland

9 ▲

ENDERBY LAND

D'Urville Sea

4 ▲

WILKES LAND

BANZARE COAST

▲13

INGRID CHRISTENSEN COAST

MACROBERTSON COAST

SABRINA COAST

KNOX COAST

QUEEN MARY COAST

7 ▲

8 ▲

INDIAN OCEAN

--- Political Boundaries

▲ 1-32 Antarctic Stations

▲ 33-36 Areas of Natural Interest

5 ▲

6 ▲

116

ANTARCTIC BASES

ANTARCTIC CRUISES

Opposite page: Antarctica has an almost circular shape, which is varied only by the Antarctic Peninsula *(enlarged in the inset)* and the two indentations of the Ross Sea and the Weddell Sea. The map indicates the antarctic bases and several of the more significant areas of natural interest in Patagonia.

The majority of the bases are set up along the coasts of the Antarctic Peninsula and are equipped by the countries that signed the Antarctic Treaty of 1959. The bases are more or less permanently active, with an involvement in scientific research. Only researchers belonging to expeditions with an authorized program are permitted access.

1) Little America (United States); 2) Scott (New Zealand); 3) McMurdo (United States); 4) Dumont d'Urville (France); 5) Wilkes (Australia); 6) Mirny (Soviet Union); 7) Davis (Australia); 8) Mawson (Australia); 9) Stowa (Japan); 10) King Baldwin (Belgium); 11) Sunae (South Africa); 12) Halley Bay (Great Britain).

13) Komsomolskaja (Soviet Union); 14) Vostok (Soviet Union); 15) Sovjetskaja (Soviet Union); 16) Novolazareskaja (Soviet Union); 17) Amundsen-Scott (United States); 18) Eights (United States).

19) Rothera (Great Britain); 20) San Martin (Argentina); 21) Faraday (Great Britain); 22) Palmer (United States); 23) Admiral Brown (Argentina); 24) Primavera (Argentina); 25) Captain Arturo Prat (Chile); 26) Vice Commodore Marambio (Argentina); 27) President Frei (Chile); 28) General Bernardo O'Higgins (Chile); 29) Bellingshausen (Soviet Union); 30) Esperanza (Argentina); 31) Arctowski (Poland); 32) Petrel (Argentina).

In theory, access to the interior of the continent of Antarctica is still reserved for the researchers at scientific bases and exploratory missions. However, for some years now it has been possible for tourists to visit the coasts and the islands.

The antarctic cruises generally leave from South America or New Zealand. They stop at the South Shetland Islands and the western coast of the continent, where they visit at Argentinian, Chilean, British, or American bases. One of the more common cruise routes includes Deception Island and its volcano, Argentina Island, Le Maire Channel, Tierra del Fuego, and sometimes the Falkland Islands.

The cruises that depart from Christ Church, New Zealand, include the Ross Sea and Ross Island. The island is dominated by the two volcanic peaks of Erebus and Terror. There are two bases on the island, McMurdo (United States) and Scott (New Zealand). Here, passengers can visit the

historic huts of the explorers Scott and Shackleton. It is possible to navigate along the glacial front of the Ross Ice Shelf for hundreds of miles. Or one might head farther north along the coast of Victoria Land to Hallet, where there are numerous colonies of penguins. These cruises operate only during the brief summer period from the end of December to mid-February. The major attractions consist of the huge tabular icebergs and the numerous antarctic animals.

Another possibility is offered by air travel. Between the end of October and the end of February, tourist flights depart from Australia and New Zealand. In one day, it is possible to admire the view from above the coasts and the icy lands of Antarctica. One can also fly over the pole.

THE FALKLANDS

The Falkland Islands cover an area of 4,632 sq. miles (12,000 sq. km) and have a human population of barely two thousand people. They are located between 51 and 53 degrees latitude south. Because of the blustering winds, there are no trees. However, there are 150 species of shrubs and green plants, including various forage grasses. Mosses and lichens are abundant.

The animals include five species of penguins, such as the king penguin, as well as elephant seals, albatrosses, cormorants, and skuas. In recent years, the native people have begun to promote tourism on the islands. This is justified by the rich natural resources of the Falklands.

SOUTH GEORGIA

This small island group covers an area of 1,449 sq. miles (3,755 sq. km) at about 55 degrees latitude south and 37 degrees longitude west. It is administered by the Falkland Islands. South Georgia has considerably fewer inhabitants than the Falklands, although it has just as many marine birds.

OTHER SOUTHERN ISLANDS

Among the other islands that are located near the Antarctic, one should mention the Sandwich Islands (east of South Georgia), the Orkneys (across from the Antarctic Peninsula), the South Shetlands (near Graham Land of the Antarctic Peninsula), Peter I Island, and Scott Island. These islands can be visited by taking an antarctic cruise. There are also ships that occasionally transport researchers from the various continental bases to the islands.

CHILE

Cape Horn (33)

This national park extends over an area of about 243 sq. miles (630 sq. km), ranging from sea level to an elevation of almost 3,280 feet (1,000 m). The park was established in 1945 on the islands of Wollastone and Hermit in the Departemiento del Tierra del Fuego, in the extreme south of Chile.

The vegetation is dominated by a dwarf forest of antarctic beech and bulbous plants. The true forest is limited to small valleys that are sheltered from the ocean wind. Along the coasts, there are numerous marine animals, such as the otter, the South American sea lion, and the southern fur seal. Among the numerous species of birds are many kelp gulls and diving petrels.

ARGENTINA

Tierra del Fuego (34)

This national park was established in 1960 over an area of 243 sq. miles (630 sq. km). Its territory has elevations that range from sea level to about 3,280 feet (1,000 m). The landscapes consist of mountains, valleys, rivers, lakes, glaciers, and a section of coast.

The vegetation includes antarctic beech forests that are rich with mosses. The larger animals include Andean deer, guanacos, South American otters, South American foxes, and, on the coast, South American sea lions, petrels, albatrosses, and penguins.

Los Glaciares (35)

This national park of 1,721 sq. miles (4,459 sq. km) was established in 1937 within an area of over 2,316 sq. miles (6,000 sq. km). The park is located in the southern Andes Mountains at the border with Chile. An area of about 594 sq. miles (1,541 sq. km) is protected as a nature reserve. There are Andean-Patagonian forests with antarctic beech, Magellan fuchsia, and winter's bark trees. There are also grasslands, snowfields, and glaciers.

The animals include the small armadillo, the Patagonian chinchilla-mouse, the mara rodent, the puma, the guanaco, the Patagonian tinamou (a primitive ground bird resembling a partridge), and the Magellan woodpecker.

Perito Francisco P. Moreno (36)

This national park of 326 sq. miles (845 sq. km) was established in 1937 within an area of 444 sq. miles (1,150 sq. km). A nature reserve occupies 117 sq. miles (305 sq. km) of the total area. The area is situated between elevations of 2,953 and 9,088 feet (900 to 2,770 m) in the northwestern part of the province of Santa Cruz.

GLOSSARY

adaptation change or adjustment by which a species or individual improves its condition in relationship to its environment.

algae primitive organisms which resemble plants but do not have true roots, stems, or leaves.

amoeba a microscopic one-celled animal found in soil and water.

amphibian any of a class of vertebrates that usually begins life in the water as a tadpole with gills and later develops lungs.

amphipod any of several crustaceans with one set of feet for jumping or walking and another set of swimming. The sand flea is an amphipod.

atmosphere the gaseous mass surrounding the earth. The atmosphere consists of oxygen, nitrogen, and other gases, and extends to a height of about 22,000 miles (35,000 km).

basin all the land drained by a river and its branches. Water collects near a basin to form lakes.

biogeography the branch of biology that deals with the geographical distribution of plants and animals.

biology the science that deals with the origin, history, physical characteristics, life processes, etc. of plant and animals.

conifers cone-bearing trees and shrubs, most of which are evergreens. Many forests are dominated by conifer trees.

conservation the controlled use and systematic protection of natural resources, such as forests and waterways.

continent one of the principal land masses of the earth. Africa, Antarctic, Asia, Europe, North America, South America, and Australia are regarded as continents.

crustacean any of a class of hard-shelled, segmented organisms that usually live in the water and breathe through gills. Shrimps, crabs, and barnacles are crustaceans.

deciduous forests forests having trees that shed their leaves at a specific season or stage of growth.

diatom any of a number of microscopic algae, one-celled or in colonies, which are a source of food for all kinds of marine life.

environment the circumstances or conditions of a plant or animal's surroundings.

epiphyte a plant, such as certain orchids or ferns, that grows on another plant upon which it depends for physical support but not for nutrients.

erosion natural processes such as weathering, abrasion, and corrosion, by which material is removed from the earth's surface.

evolution a gradual process in which something changes into a different and usually more complex or better form.

filament a very slender thread or fiber.

fiord a narrow inlet or arm of the sea bordered by steep cliffs.

fossil a remnant or trace of an organism of a past geologic age, such as a skeleton or leaf imprint, embedded in some part of the earth's crust. Scientists search for fossils as a way of learning about past life.

geology the science dealing with the physical nature and history of the earth. Geology includes a study of the structure and development of the earth's crust, the composition of its interior, individual types of rock, and the forms of life which can be found.

glaciers gigantic moving sheets of ice that covered great areas of the earth in an earlier time. Glaciers existed primarily in the Pleistocene period, one million years ago.

habitat the area or type of environment in which a person or other organism normally occurs.

hemisphere any of the halves of the earth. The earth is divided by the equator into the Northern and Southern hemispheres and by a meridian into the Eastern and Western hemispheres.

humid containing a large amount of water or water vapor.

larva the early, immature form of any animal that changes structurally when it becomes an adult.

lichen a primitive plant formed by the association of blue-green algae with fungi.

mammal any of a large class of warm-blooded, usually hairy vertebrates whose offspring are fed with milk secreted from special glands in the female.

mollusk an invertebrate animal characterized by a soft, usually unsegmented body, often enclosed in a shell, and having gills and a foot. Oysters, clams, and snails are mollusks.

oasis any fertile place in a desert, due to the presence of water.

organism any individual animal or plant having diverse organs and parts that function as a whole to maintain life and its activities.

ornithology the branch of zoology dealing with birds.

paleontology the branch of geology that deals with prehistoric forms of life through the study of plant and animal fossils.

parasite an organism that grows, feeds, and is sheltered on or in a different organism while contributing nothing to the survival of its host.

peninsula a land area almost entirely surrounded by water and connected to the mainland by a narrow strip of earth called an isthmus.

photosynthesis the process by which chlorophyll-containing cells in green plants convert sunlight into chemical energy and change inorganic into organic compounds.

phytoplankton small, floating aquatic plants. Phytoplankton is formed by huge quantities of microscopic algae adrift in the water, and thrives only if sunlight filters through the water, allowing for photosynthesis.

protozoan any of a group of mostly microscopic animals made up of a single cell or a group of more or less identical cells and living chiefly in water.

salinity of or relating to the saltiness of something. The salinity of ocean water, for instance, varies in different regions and depths.

shrub a low, woody plant with several permanent stems instead of a single trunk; a bush.

species a distinct kind, sort, variety, or class. Plant and animal species have a high degree of similarity and can generally interbreed only among themselves.

temperate a climate which is neither very color nor very hot, but rather moderate.

tundra a treeless area between the icecap and the tree line of arctic regions, having a permanently frozen subsoil. The tundra can support only low-lying vegetation such as lichens, mosses, and stunted shrubs.

xerophyte a plant structurally adapted to growing under very dry or desert conditions, often having smaller leaf surfaces for avoiding water loss, thick fleshy parts for water storage, and hairs, spines, or thorns.

zooplankton floating, often microscopic sea animals. Zooplankton is eaten by many organisms, including the anchovy.

INDEX

CREDITS

MAPS AND DRAWINGS. G. Vaccaro, Cologna Veneta (Verona, Italy). **PHOTOGRAPHS. L. Boitani,** Rome: 41, 74. **B. Lanza,** Florence: 96, 100-101, 104-105, 107, 112-113. **Overseas,** Milan: E. Mickleburg, 8, 13, 14-15, 22-23, 90; Jacana/F. Gohier 64-65; Photo Credit/Ocean Films/A. Giddings 68-69; Oxford Scientific Films/D. Allan 59, 62-63. **Panda Photo,** Rome: D. Allan cover, 10-11, 17, 21, 27, 28-29, 42, 43, 44, 54, 55, 60, 72, 75, 76-77, 78-79, 81, 83, 88-89, 93, 94-95, 120-121; ENEA Progetto Antartide/M. Frezzotti 33, 34-35, 118. **L. Pellegrini,** Milan: 6-7, 24, 36-37, 38, 47, 48-49, 86, 103, 108-109, 110-111, 114.

DATE DUE

Printed
in USA